HER FIGHT | HIS BATTLE

Finding the Beauty of Hope,
in the Midst of Unbeautiful Seasons

LISA ADAMS

WESTBOW
PRESS®
A DIVISION OF THOMAS NELSON
& ZONDERVAN

WestBow Press books may be ordered through booksellers or by contacting:

WestBow Press
A Division of Thomas Nelson & Zondervan
1663 Liberty Drive
Bloomington, IN 47403
www.westbowpress.com
844-714-3454

Cover Design: *Lisa Adams*
Interior Layout: *Lisa Adams*

ISBN: 978-1-6642-4554-9 (sc)
ISBN: 978-1-6642-4555-6 (e)

Print information available on the last page.

WestBow Press rev. date: 09/20/2022

NOTE TO THE READER

Thank you for reading this book. This book is written with love, appreciation, and gratefulness to the Almighty Creator of Heaven and Earth and everything in it. This book is filled with alerts, analogies, poetry, prayers, quotes, Scriptures, and tells a basic story. Each *Season* starts with a Scripture. Each **chapter** has a forecast summary at the end that depicts what is happening in that particular *Season* and the pivotal points of what the author would need to heed going forward into the next *Season*. Wherever you see anything **bolded** or a word *Capitalized* with *Italics,* it is to emphasize a point of reference; or what was precious to me during these *Seasons.*

Take a walk with me through various *Seasons* in my life where events crash into beautiful colors that collide into a purposeful destiny. May you enjoy the read!

Blessings

Lisa

APPRECIATION

The Whispers of a Mother's Love

Mom,
My guardian angel,
you softly spoke these precious words to me:
"And this too shall pass!"
Mere words cannot express
my heartfelt appreciation,
of your unconditional
whispers of love!

Forever loving you,
Lisa

CONTENTS

Fall Equinox: Climate, Change, and Colors

Season Cast Synopsis:

Seasons Cast: Emancipation, Extraordinaire, Expectation, and Enlightened!

PROLOGUE

Uncertain Seasons

There is a time for everything,
and a SEASON for every activity under the heavens:
. . . He has made everything beautiful in its time . . .
Ecclesiastes 3:1 & 3:11a (NIV)

Beautiful! Strikingly beautiful! When I think of the words strikingly beautiful; I think about the intricate colors and designs of the butterfly. The butterfly is one of God's most beautiful creations. Many people marvel at the butterfly's majestic burst of colors; but rarely stop to appreciate the life cycle journey of that majestic splendor. Their majestic splendor emerges from a cute-ugly caterpillar. The cute-ugly caterpillar goes through four basic life cycles (egg, caterpillar, chrysalis, butterfly) similarly this book is based on four different *Seasons* (*Winter, Spring, Summer, and Fall*). Each *Season* tells a story and gives voice to the current life cycle within that *Season* (see chart below).

Life Cycle of Butterfly	Life Cycle Seasons	Life Cycle Outcomes
Egg	Winter | Dormant	Obstinate Obstacles
Caterpillar	Spring | Hope	Optimistic Opportunity
Chrysalis | Pupa	Summer | Struggle	Turbulent Troubles
Butterfly	Fall | Restoration	Testimonial Triumphs

My voice, in the beginning, is from a **victor's cry** which emerged from the harrowing depth of my angst and pains. The angst and pains were captured and canvas with broad strokes upon my heart, mind, body, and soul. Some of these experiences were welcoming and picturesque; while others were filled with the agony of unwelcoming throes. These unwelcoming throes took me on an uncertain journey that became an unforgettable experience! God used these *Seasons* to transform my cute-ugly-caterpillar circumstances into a beautiful-bold-butterfly that would ultimately represent a **victor's crown**!

God's unconditional loving-kindness has shown me that: *He has made everything beautiful in its time*—Ecclesiastes 3:11 (NIV).

FORECAST

Today is cloudy with beaming sun rays peeking through the curtains of puffy white clouds. The temperature high is 68 degrees of beautifulness, with a chance of a 50% increase of pure awesomeness, coupling towards 100% warmth of loving-kindness! A mild wind will sweep in with a sweet calming peace, along with joyful happiness, as the rays of sunshine touch down upon all who are open to receiving the message.

———⚬⚬⚬———

Every message sent is not necessarily a message that you may want to hear, yet it is a message that you would need to heed.

WINTER SOLSTICE
Frosty, Freezing, and Frigid

*Sustain me, my God, according to your promise, and
I will live; do not let my hopes be dashed.*
Psalm 119:116 (NIV)

Have you ever wanted to tell someone something sooooo bad that you could not wait to share it with them? When you see the person, you make a beeline towards the individual to share your fantabulous news. You find yourself brimming over with excitement from the anticipation of their supportive response. You begin to share anddddd—you are aghast as you stop mid-sentence at their hard-hearted ice-cold response. You are taken aback! Their response has stunned you silent! Instantly, their ice-glazed frigid facial expression sends an irritated chill through your body.

You think to yourself, "what just happened?" You are at a loss for words. You and this pessimistic polar arctic type personality do not share the same sentiments about your fantabulous news. You try to shake off their negativity, yet their frigid reaction continues to slide down the wintry slopes of your mind. You begin to second-guess your fantabulous news. You wonder about the individual's response. You wonder whether your delivery was correct. You wonder whether the person is having a bad day. You wonder, you wonder and you wonder. Like the wheels of wonderment spinning in your head, you wonder again if you should have kept this fantabulous news to yourself.

Yet, in your heart of hearts, you know that - - that is an impossibility. Your heart is full to overflow and bursting at the seams to release this awesome fantabulous news. This news was too beautiful to contain. I wondered who could I find to share with me in this delight—hmmmmm.

My mood pendulum swung from hot hopefulness to lukewarm doubtfulness, and then forcefully thrust into cold-hearted callousness. I was trying not to allow my happy place with God to become frozen with hopelessness. As one author stated:

"Hope is truly hard to find with frost-bitten fingers."

ALERT: The *Winter Season* brings meteorological conditions that come through various atmospheric pressures. These pressures are different for each individual. If you are unable to grasp this message, it is because you are clearly in a *Wintery Season*, snowbound with a lack of understanding. The one constant about the *Winter Season* is that you will need a thick coat of clarity, coupled with the hat of understanding, along with a snug pair of gloves for knowledge and discernment. Brrrrrrrr—you feel that? It is *Winter*—and it is sooooo very cold!

FORECAST

The air pressure is set to pique an outlook range of bold beautiful blue skies. Yet, clouds will swiftly move in and bring a Wintery storm severity index with dewdrops of freezing rain that will chill the air and tickle the frost upon your nose. Gusty winds and dropped temperatures will produce harsh hailstorms.

Everyone is not on the same page or walking on the same path. Sometimes you will have to walk your journey alone. The journey can get very lonely and make you feel a bit frosty. Don't get stuck in the freeze-zone, locate the deicer and proceed with caution.

Season beginnings
'Tis the Unpredictable Seasons of Pain!

Uncompromising Season

THE PASSION

One beautiful *Summer* day I took a road trip with some friends (Adriana, Connie, Rochelle) to Charleston, South Carolina—specifically James Island. On the way down we talked and laughed and just had a good ole happy sing-along riding fun girl time. When we arrived in South Carolina, the South Carolinians extended the most gracious hospitality and the food was delicious. I had never heard of anyone eating shrimp and grits—what a delicious concept. On the drive back, Connie and Rochelle fell asleep in the back of the truck while Adriana and I began an unforgettable conversation.

Our conversation flowed. We talked about any and everything. I could not quite put my finger on it, but it was something about this woman that kept pricking at my senses. Suddenly it hit me; the same presence I was feeling at this moment was the same presence that I felt with a co-worker name Theresa in a similar conversation about fifteen years ago. This in itself intrigued me. Somehow, I instinctively knew that these two beautiful women were of one in the same *Spirit*. Neither one of these two women knew each other. What stood out for me was that neither of them mentioned Jesus. They never profess a religion or uttered a religious expression, which is the norm in the Christian faith. Not once did either of them say Praise God! Not once did either of them say Glory, Hallelujah, or Amen during our conversation—yet without knowing if either were Christians, something in me felt the need to ask both of them the same question, "are you **saved**?"

Now let me be clear, I truly did not know what I was asking. Yet, those were the words that tumbled out of my mouth both times with each woman. I had no idea what **saved** meant. I remembered in the **Bible** that Jesus asked Peter a question . . . *who do you say that I am . . . You are the Christ, the Son of the living God . . . Jesus answered . . . flesh and blood has not revealed this to you, but My Father who is in heaven*—Matthew 16:15–18 (MEV). I can truly understand this because I had no idea what **saved** meant, or why I asked that question at that time since no mention of God or anything godly had been a part of either conversation. Ironically, they both responded in the same manner with great joy as if I had just asked a million-dollar question. They both expounded on the greatness and the love of God. My spirit was too immature to understand the depth of what I just asked. I do not remember verbatim what they said but the writings of their beautiful spirits were etched upon my heart, without me even knowing it.

As we continued the drive from South Carolina back to Maryland, I kept thinking how unique and also how uncanny it was that I felt the presence of the same *Spirit* with both women and that I felt the need to ask them both the same question concerning being **saved.** This brought into remembrance the Scripture—Ephesians 4:4 (CSB) that states: *There is one body, and one Spirit.* This would become very real to me as I matured in Christ. The similarities in their conversations had me intrigued. Adriana and Theresa talked about God with great love and that puzzled me because they both had lost their moms. I could not understand how they loved a God who took their mom from them. I asked them both the same question concerning their mother: "How do you love God when He killed your mother?" Neither one of them was annoyed at my ignorance but answered me with loving-kindness and continued expounding on their great love for the Most-High God. I was intrigued with their complete devotion to God despite their circumstances.

I could not fathom this type of love. Their love for God was puzzling, yet at the same time, it had piqued my interest. The more Adriana talked about God, with passion and fervor, the more I desired to have what she had with God, which unbeknownst to me at that time was a relationship.

When we got back from our road trip, Adriana started a Purpose Driven Life (PDL) **Bible** study group. The Purpose Driven Life is a book written by Pastor Rick Warren of Saddleback Church. I will never forget our very first **Bible** study meeting nor the very first sentence on the very first page of the book (PDL) that simply stated:

"It is not about you."

I immediately voiced my two cents of knowledge by emphatically stating with the arm gestures and bouncy eyes: "Of course it is about me; who else would it be about, duh?" Eyes stared back at me as if I had said something absurd. I decided to take a chill pill and let that topic go, thus I backed down. I thought to myself, from now on I will keep my opinions to myself since everyone was looking at me as if I had just made the most ludicrous statement of all times. I kept thinking to myself: "What's wrong with these people?" I decided to let them think whatever they wanted to think since it was obvious that they were clueless! After all, I reasoned that people have the right to think whatever they want, even if their thoughts made no sense to me at the time.

We took turns having the **Bible** study at each other's homes. I must admit, this was one of the best **Bible** studies I had ever attended. Well, it was the first up-close-and-personal **Bible** study I had ever attended. The dialogue went very deep and was genuinely profound. I began to understand some things and re-think other things. For reasons that were not apparent to me at the time, I began to have a thirst for God. I could not get enough of what I was learning. I needed to get a **Bible**. I had no idea there were so many versions. I found it difficult to read the King James Version (KJV). I was elated to find the New International Version (NIV), which was easier for me to understand at that time.

One weekend our **Bible** study was at Adriana's house. The study was intriguing as always. Adriana was a great teacher. I excused myself and went to the powder room. I saw a picture hanging on the wall that immediately captured my attention. Instantly, something was stirred in me. I just knew I had to write this Scripture down and I did so without hesitation. It was like the words had taken a hold of me. I could not - - not write them down. Thus, pen to paper, I wrote down the Scripture of Proverbs 3:5–6 (NKJV): *Trust in the Lord with all your heart, and lean not on your understanding; In all your ways acknowledge Him, and He shall direct your path.*

As the **Bible** study was coming to a close for the evening, we gathered in a circle and took each other's hands. Adriana was about to lead us into prayer and said:

"Since we are all **saved**,"

I stopped her mid-sentence and said, "What do you mean when you say **saved**?" Now, remember I mentioned earlier that I had no idea what **saved** meant. This was the proof in the pudding that I had no idea what the word **saved** meant. Her response was:

"If you have to ask, then you are probably not **saved**."

She explained what it meant to be **saved** and asked me if I wanted to be **saved**. I expressed my consent and I accepted Jesus Christ into my life. As she prayed over me, I could hear the sounds of oceans in my ears and I could not stop crying. This was in January 2005. I believe the reason Proverbs 3:5–6 is my favorite Scripture is because the same day I saw that Scripture; God tugged at my heart, I surrendered, and I embraced the gift of *Salvation.*

Like a newbie Christian, I was riding the wave of cloud nine and feeling very good. To say I was thirsty for the *Word of God* would be an understatement. I had an unquenchable thirst for *His Word*, which led me to purchase **my first Bible**. I craved the *Word of God* and ventured to read the **Bible** from beginning to end. I had never read the **Bible** cover to cover nor did I even own a **Bible**. I was amazed at how much revelation was packed in the **Bible**.

I fell in love with the New International Version and toted it with me the majority of the time. This was my favorite **Bible** version. I would read it on the train, bus, car, or wherever. I could never seem to get enough. I carried the **Bible** in a black zip-around leather binder casing. In this leather binder, I had highlighted Scriptures with color-coded post-it-tabs, affirmations, and encouraging notes. My **Bible** was so organized that I could do a search on the colored-coded post-it tabs for a specific topic. For example, the yellow flags referenced light or sun/Son, or red flags love/Jesus and so forth and so on. This was my go-to favorite binder. **I loved my Bible and my Bible binder carrying case!** Anything that I came across that touched me in some way, shape, or form, went into that **Bible binder carrying case**.

As any seeker, I had lots of questions. There was so much I did not understand. There would be many times when I would be looking from my perspective and I would miss the understanding. I had not learned how to look from the purview of God. God was working with me on learning to trust Him. As well as teaching me to tame my mind and tongue from being super judgmental and overly critical. At times, I would assume that I had removed the judgment hat, but God would show me that it was still there, it was just cocked to the side. The journey of learning not to judge nor to be supercritical was not easy. I cannot tell you how many tests I had failed. God gave me a word that I still remember to this day. He simply said:

"Love and not judge."

I grappled with the concept of learning to love and not judge. To embrace this concept, I had to hide Scriptures in my heart such as: *Do not depend on your own understanding*—Proverbs 3:5 (NLT).

Over time I became truly grateful for the lessons that were disguised as obstacles but were blessings. God was showing me that every picture had an inner and outer picture that expounded on the true picture. I learned that we cannot completely draw from the surface of a picture without understanding what lies beneath the interior, or what has infected the exterior. Trusting God for what I could not see would become a pivotal point in our relationship. As I sought God through a personal one-on-one relationship; more and more was revealed to me. One such revelation for the aforementioned *Women of God* were:

> Theresa planted the seed,
> Adriana watered the seed,
> and Purpose Driven Life fed the seed!

In Ecclesiastes 3:1 (NIV), it states: *There is a time for everything, and a Season for every activity under the heavens.* Everything is divinely orchestrated, even if we do not realize it or understand this statement. I was enjoying my newfound relationship with God to the max. I was on fire for God and I wanted everyone to know what I was experiencing. Yet, I found out quickly, that everyone did not want to hear about my fantabulous news. This perplexed me because I thought this was the best news ever! I could not help but wonder why other people did not want this same experience.

I began studying and memorizing Scripture. Every time that I came across a Scripture that touched me, I would either highlight it or write it down to be tucked away into my beloved **Bible** binder case. I was super happy with the journey that I was pursuing with God. I knew God loved me and I loved Him! But His Grace—need I say more! The whole concept of grace is mind-boggling. It is the most outrageous, most indescribable, most unjustifiable gift ever. It is true reckless abandonment! The inexpressible gift of grace can be likened to a precious priceless jewel. I was appreciative of this beautiful jewel of grace from God. Just knowing that my sins were completely forgiven, my filth completely washed away, and that God completely loves me despite them meant more to me than anyone could ever begin to imagine.

I was on fire for God! The prophet Jeremiah and I spoke the same sentiments when he said: *For the word of the LORD has become for me . . . a burning fire shut up in my bones*—Jeremiah 20:8–9 (ESV). My excitement and love for God could not be contained. Nothing, and I do mean nothing was going to ever turn me back from my walk with God. No, nothing, not anyone ever! Never! Ever! Ever!

There is an out-of-control fire burning that cannot be
put out in the mountain forest of God's love!

───── ∞∞ ─────

When a fire is kindled in your heart it is important to fuel the fire with the Word of God, surround yourself with the people of God, and stay connected to the places of God; otherwise, your fire will be quickly smothered.

Unguarded Season

THE PROBLEM

I was flying high in my relationship with God. Life was good! All was well! I could not be happier than I was during this time. I was on cloud nine and singing His praises. And then the phone rang, ring, ring, ring:

> "Hello, this is the doctor's office; we are calling concerning your mammogram and we would like to schedule a time for you to come back in to have another one done."

An alarm began to blare in my head. The doctor's office never calls. They always send a letter in the U.S. (United States) postal mail indicating that the mammogram was negative and that they would see me next year. I had been taking this test for years and I had never received a telephone call. Nevertheless, they scheduled a date for me to come into the radiology department to retake the mammogram. I tried not to worry; however, the fact that they called, gave me reasons to pause.

I was shifting with worry as I was waiting on the results from the second mammogram, all while trying to trust God. I remembered my beloved favorite Scripture in Proverbs and I tried to wrap my mind around it to keep me from building up anxiety. As I was uttering the words: *Trust in the Lord with all your heart and lean not* . . . (Proverbs 3:5 NIV), the phone rang, ring, ring, ring:

> "Hello, this is the doctor's office, the results of the second mammogram are in and we would like to schedule a time to meet and discuss the results."

Silence! What do you say when you get a call like this?

> "Hello?"

The person on the line was aware of the eerie silence that was now apparent. "I am here," I responded. Talking about taking the joy right out of your life. I felt like a balloon that had just been popped. The telephone call had sucked all the energy out of me. I was speechless, this is not something I was ever anticipating or expecting. Yet, the unexpected had not only shown up, but it had also set me on a path to fret continuously. I knew that the doctor's office would be calling; however, the phone call took me by surprise. I could not shake the fear of the possibility. I did not want to say the c-word. Just thinking about it made me a nervous wreck. I could not stop my runaway mind from these thoughts. I could not shake the heaviness. The weight of fear hovered over me like a helicopter shining the spotlight on its victim. I simply could not stop worrying.

I arrived at the doctor's office with dread enveloping me like it was my best friend. The doctor told me that they looked at both mammograms and the same spot showed up. I was told that I needed to have a biopsy done so that they can take a sampling of the tumor. The biopsy was unsuccessful because the tumor was deeply embedded in my chest cavity and the needle could not reach the targeted area. Thus, the doctor scheduled an MRI (Magnetic Resonance Imaging) in order to get an accurate assessment of the tumor. I was told the MRI would precisely point out the invaded area so that the surgeon would be able to extract part of the tumor to make an accurate diagnosis.

My mom and I pulled into the MRI Center parking area. The wait was not long and before I knew it, they were calling my name. The radiology technician showed me a closed capsule that I would have to enter, and I instantaneously was taken aback and became devastated. I shared my fears with the radiology technician who was explaining the process to me. I was thinking to myself, there was no way that I was going into that capsule for one minute, let alone thirty minutes. I have always been claustrophobic—for goodness sakes! I began to cry uncontrollably. The radiology technician tried to calm me down with some pills, which I was later told were sugar pills. I had always been claustrophobic so how in the world was this MRI going to take place. I asked if there were any other options. The response was:

"Sweetie, this is your last option because the biopsy was unsuccessful."

I tried to gather my nerves because they were all over the place. I laid out on the MRI table and closed my eyes. The radiology technician began putting me into the capsule. My first mistake was opening my eyes. I cannot say I lasted 10 seconds. I began to shout and wiggle in the capsule. I had to get out of there! She calmly said:

"It's okay, please calm down, I am getting you out now."

I could not get out of there fast enough. I did not know what to do. I felt like my last hope had just gone out the window. The radiology technician was trying to calm me down. I checked out of that conversation and instantly began a heartfelt prayer cry to God. With tear-streaked eyes, I earnestly prayed to God for His help. I whispered to God: "I cannot do this and if You don't do this, it won't get done!" I tune my mind back to what the radiology technician was saying to me. She was explaining the importance of getting the MRI done. The radiologist said:

"Let's try it again."

I simply said, "okay." But God! And I do mean, but God! I had prayed to God that if He did not do it, it would not get done. I went into the capsule with a peace that made absolutely no sense. I finally understood what is meant by the phrase: *Peace. . . that surpasses all understanding*—Philippian 4:7 (NKJV). I was overwhelmed with gratefulness. The Scripture, Proverbs 3:5 (NKJV): *Trust in the Lord* continually played on my heartstrings while inside the capsule. I recited it over and over again until the radiology technician pulled me out.

I was in there for thirty minutes and never felt claustrophobic—not once, never panicked—not once, never felt unease—not once. I cannot explain it. I knew I had just witnessed a miracle! But God, it was an instantaneous miracle! God showed up that day and I had so much joy in my heart and peace in my soul that I could not stop thanking Him for the miracle that I had just witnessed. I left the MRI on cloud nine, continually praising and thanking God. No one could tell me that God did not love me—after what He had just done. I knew without a doubt that God loved this daughter. Again, there is nothing like a sincere thank you praise and I could not stop thanking and praising Him! God had delivered me in a big way and I was overly appreciative. At that moment, I loved God and I knew God loved me.

I went to the doctor's office to discuss the test results of the MRI and was told that I would have to have surgery to determine whether the tumor was benign or malignant. I did not want to consider the test being anything other than benign. I was frightened to have surgery. On the day of surgery, I got up early and could not go back to sleep. I was so afraid to go into the surgery for fear of some erroneous error occurring that I would go into a coma or die. I cried out to God and told Him about my fears. I asked Him for a Word to get me through this ordeal. I was a frantic mess! I could not seem to get it together as I continued crying out to God. I was beyond scared. I went and got my **Bible** binder that I loved so much. I asked God to please speak to me because I desperately needed to hear from Him.

I opened up the **Bible** and my eyes landed on Isaiah 41:10 (NIV):

Do not fear, for I am with you. I just about lost it. God miraculously answered me instantaneously once again. I was so happy because I knew God had just answered my prayer. That Scripture changed my entire mood because I knew God had heard me. Just knowing that God would be there gave me a calming peace. I thanked Him profusely. After thanking Him for answering me, I sent up another request and asked God to put His angels all around me today.

I arrived at the Surgical Center with my **Bible** binder case that I loved in tow. The front desk called my name and fear crept up on me. Every time fear arose in me, I would bring to remembrance the Scripture that He gave me that morning, Isaiah 41:10 (NIV): *Do not fear, for I am with you.* As the day progressed, I was still nervous, but I truly believed without a shadow of a doubt that God was with me because that is what He said to me that morning. The receptionist must have read my face because she looked directly at me and said:

"It is going to be okay, there are angels all around you."

Now, this is not something I would expect a receptionist or any worker in a secular hospital to say. I knew God was hearing me today because He just confirmed my second request via the receptionist that angels were all around me. It felt good to know that God heard my prayer and was placing angels all around me. Knowing that God was with me, gave me a needed semblance of peace.

I returned to my seat and sat down. My name was called once again, but this time it was to go to the back to prepare for the surgery. Fear tried to sneak up on me. I pushed that thought out of my head and focused on the Scripture that God had given to me that morning; Isaiah 41:10 (NIV): *Do not fear, for I am with you.* I sat down, and the nurse must have observed my nervousness because she said:

"Take this pill, you will be fine. I know this is your first surgery but remember there are angels all around you."

Once again, my prayers were affirmed concerning the angels. As the anesthesiologist came and introduced himself, fear began yelling—I'm back. I intentionally pushed that fear to the side and forced myself to concentrate on the Scripture that God had spoken to me that morning—Isaiah 41:10 (NIV): *Do not fear, for I am with you.* I began to repeat the Scripture over and over again: *Do not fear, for I am with you. Do not fear, for I am with you. Do not fear, for I am . . .* —Isaiah 41:10 (NIV). Only God, only God, only God! I do not remember going to sleep. I woke up in recovery as if nothing ever happened. I thanked God for a successful surgery. They scheduled me for my follow-up appointment before I left the surgical center.

My follow-up appointment had me rethinking my life. I was told that I had breast cancer and it was aggressively malignant. The doctor said they needed to get me immediately into surgery because of the aggressiveness of this particular cancer. Sadness surrounded me as I began slipping into a dark space of depression. Death was peeking through the keyhole of my heart and trying to stake its fear into the depths of my soul. Slowly, I began spiraling down into worry and fear. I could not shake these feelings. I did not want to talk to anyone anymore. I did not know what I was going to tell my family, kids, friends, or job.

I had not been a Christian for any real length of time, I was a newbie for goodness' sake. How could He do this to me? I did not want to read the **Bible** anymore. God had let me down. God did not answer my prayer this time. He allowed me to have breast cancer. I could not believe He would do this to me. I thought He loved me! I thought I was the apple of His eye! How did this happen? Why did this happen? Am I a bad person? Why me? I thought He took care of His children! Me! His daughter! Right? I could not figure this out. Nothing was making sense to me anymore. I did not like the feeling of helplessness. I became dismal and withdrawn. I wanted my health back. I began to get very angry. My fear and depression turned to rage and fury. And I knew exactly what I needed to do next.

There is a severe Tropical Storm coming off of the
Gulf Coast that appears to be turning into a
Category One Hurricane . . . I need to take
refuge in the Shadows of the Almighty!

———⌘———

When problems announced themselves, create an equation and solve them!

Unforeseeable Season

THE PURSUIT

I became unhinged, disoriented, and befuddled about this diagnosis. I simply could not wrap my mind around all that was happening to me. I started thinking maybe I got the whole Christian thing wrong. I became angrier and angrier and angrier. I needed to disconnect from this Christian life. I did not have any of these issues until I became a Christian. How does a good God allow evil things to take hold of His children? Clearly, this good God did not quite understand what the word good meant.

I was done with God and the whole Christianity fiasco. Simply because I was appalled at what He was allowing to happen in my life. I knew He was God, and He could do anything so as far as I was concerned, He could change this situation right now. But it was clear that He did not want to do that. I did not understand why He wanted me to suffer. He was not being a nice God after all. I had it all wrong. My mind was now made up and I was done with Christianity. If all this affliction is because I am a Christian, then this life is not for me. Who wants to suffer? Not me! I needed to sever my ties with Christians who

I felt had just set me up! I was preparing my exit plan and to take flight like a 747 and ping went the sound of a new email.

Ping, an email popped in from Adriana. I mulled over the email and was deciding if I should answer or ignore it. I opened the email, and it was friendly enough, but I needed to flee from these people because my life was taking a turn for the worse and I blamed them. You may think that that was silly, immature, or insane, but that is exactly where my mind was at the time. I was wrestling with myself and trying to determine how I should respond to her. I decided that I would be upfront with her. I told her that I was done with the whole Christianity fiasco. I told her that before I became **"saved,"** my life was great, and my health was superb. I went on to say that since I became a Christian, I got breast cancer as if someone can catch it. Looking back, I amazed myself at the words that spilled forth from my lips. I told her that I did not want anything to do with any Christians anymore. Her only comment back to me was:

"Can I call you?'

I hesitated as I pondered how to respond. After a couple of minutes of deliberation, I responded to her and gave her my work phone number. She replied in the email:

"I am calling you right now."

Adriana greeted me with niceties and I responded with the same sentiments. She asked where I worked and I told her. She asked was there a restaurant nearby and I affirmed that there was one in my building. Then she said:

"Meet me there, I am on my way!"

That was the extent of our conversation, it was the quickest conversation I had ever had with her and her urgency puzzled me. I thought to myself, she can come down here all she wants but my mind is made up. And no one or nothing would change that. She could not make me stay a Christian. I did like her and I thought she was a very nice person, but nothing she could say to me would change the fact that I have breast cancer and that God is not who I thought He was. My mind, however, was made up. Her coming down to my job would be a clear waste of time. There was nothing and I do mean nothing that she could say to me that would fix the fact that I have breast cancer. And to make matters worse—it was a malignant, destructive, aggressive cancer, that could annihilate quickly—hence the speeding up of the upcoming surgery to have it removed. I thought to myself, really God—you would do this to me! I did not want to talk to God anymore. I declared—I'm done!

We met up at the restaurant and placed our orders. We exchanged greetings and made the usual small talk. I wanted to get my spiel on how I felt about Christianity over and done with so that we can move on to a different topic. I decided to let Adriana know off the back that my mind was made up. I began with how my life was great before the whole **"save thingy."** My health was perfect, and I have the medical records to prove it. I continued by letting her know that I need to get back to my old way of life where I had optimal health. I had no blemishes on my health records for forty-plus years. I was the perfect model of health and even the doctors agreed. I continued by letting her know that my doctor said to me:

> "I sure hate that I have to tarnish your record. I have never seen anyone with an unblemished record history like yours at this age. There is generally at least one thing on someone's record by the time they reach this age."

I went on to tell her that there was too much turmoil being hurled my way. How coincidental that these issues would arise now. At the time that I am pouring out my heart and studying the *Word of God*. At the time when I was desiring a relationship with God. At the time where I was desiring to pray more. At the time when I thought God loved me. Who was I kidding? Why would a God who loved me, allow death to walk up and ring my doorbell? Hello? There is nothing you or anyone can say to me about Christianity! Not you nor Your God (with stern emphasis)!

And before I could continue this sweet beautiful calm *Woman of God* interjected and stopped me mid-sentence. She was looking at me, but not talking directly to me. It was something I had never seen nor experienced before and it was something I would never forget. I saw the *Woman of God* begin warring in the Spirit. I looked at her in amazement and bewilderment simultaneously. She took authority by the *Word of God*. At that time, I did not understand what was happening nor what she was doing. I just simply stared in wonderment.

I witnessed firsthand the double-edged sword that the **Bible** talks about. I witnessed firsthand how *His Word* was the truth. I witnessed as the lies crashed to the ground. Just as the **Bible** reminds us in the book of Jeremiah 23:29 (ESV): *Is not my word like fire, declares the LORD, and like a hammer that breaks the rock in pieces?* I watched her shatter the lies that were not of God. I witnessed firsthand what it felt like to have the shackles broken. I witnessed firsthand that God had purposefully sent an angel (Adriana) after me because that was just how much He loved me. The turning point for me was that the *Love of God* had chased me down and kept me when I did not even realize that I needed to be kept. He loved me enough to come after me when I was turning my back on Him. When the warring stopped, I realized that God sent Adriana to bring me back into His loving arms. He took the time to go after the one lost sheep. I simply needed to know that He was there for me, that He cared for me, and above all that He loved me. I cannot begin to tell you how much it meant that God, the Almighty Creator of Heaven and Earth came after me—His daughter! My heartstrings were once again turned back to God and I began to pursue Him again, this time with full force and earnest trust. God sent His angel after this hopelessly lost sheep and that touched my heart tremendously. God sees our heart and God knows what we need and exactly when we need it. I thank God for coming after me! I thank God for coming after me! I will say it again, I thank God for coming after me!

I realized how quickly we can forget the things that God has done for us when things do not go our way. I had completely dismissed the two miracles that God had done before all this had happened. I had dismissed the instantaneous healing of claustrophobia and the immediate answer from God through *His Word*.

The **Bible** became my ultimate resource where I would meet with God daily. God had gifted me with His love, through the **Bible**. I was learning to stand on His unerring Word! I desired to memorize His unadulterated truth. In God's truth, there is nothing toxic, no imperfections, no impurities, and no flaws. God's truth had mounted up in my soul and lifted me to a higher love in Him. *His Word* became a medicinal healing balm for my soul.

God's grace showed me that trust would be the ultimate treasure I would need to have my soul rest upon. Trust is difficult when all the evidence says otherwise. I desired to put my complete trust in God believing that there had to be a bigger purpose for my situation in this *Season*. Yet, trials have a way of tripping you up and making you second-guess what you say you believe.

Learning to trust God, would become my deepest and toughest growing pang. In this *Wintery Season*, I needed to have faith and I needed to anchor my hope in Him. I needed to hold onto my trust in God throughout this blistery storm brewing.

FORECAST

Partly cloudy with a heavy downpour of rain that
will cause flash flood warnings for the area. Proceed
with caution and stay on Grace Lane!

Every obstacle is an opportunity for your faith to kick in and Trust God!

SPRING EQUINOX
Birds, Butterflies, and Blossoms

. . . He breathes on Winter—suddenly it's Spring!
Psalms 147:18 (MSG)

Spring bursts forth with new beginnings, new opportunities, new ideas, and new concepts. *Spring* marches forth with a pep in its step. In the *Spring*, beautiful birds are chirping, flowers bud and bloom, and butterflies hatch from their chrysalis. Alternatively, *Spring* can also bring forth adversity, obstacles, and pangs such as weeds, allergies, or health challenges.

In the *Spring*, butterflies emerge from their cocoon, similarly, we can emerge into our discovery of God. The amazing thing about the butterfly is that if you try to assist it in any way other than allowing it to break free on its' own, you will cripple its life forever. Likewise, if you do not learn to break free from the world to study the *Word of God*, with God (in a relationship), you will do a disservice to yourself by crippling your relationship with God! Your relationship with God is uniquely designed and may be completely different than someone else. Building upon a relationship with God will propel you to heights that you could never imagine.

Additionally, *Spring Seasons* are also equated with greenery, planting, and blooming. There will be many people who will sow seeds of goodness, love, and wisdom, alternatively; there will be those who throw stones that can make us become discouraged, bitter, or distrustful. The best defense is recognizing that the afflictions in your *Spring Season* are disguised as your best opportunities to grow. The best lesson anyone can learn is to never run from a *Season*; always embrace it, no matter how tough. Every *Season* will have a purpose in your life. Believe it or not, this is exactly where you need to be. And, at the appropriate time, God will bloom you right where you are planted, so be still my budding flower and expect your blossoms to bloom to their fullest potential.

ALERT: Has your appointed *Season* arrived? Are you budding? Are you walking in your purpose? If not, check the soil—it may need to be tilled!

FORECAST

Sunny and high in the upper 70s. It is the perfect *Season* for planting and tilling the gardens of your mind.

Find your garden hose of knowledge, the spade of wisdom, snips of discernment, and manage your fields before the weeds come in to take over.

Unanswered Season

THE PLEA

How do you find relief to an unanswered question that directly affects your life? There is only one source of life and I decided to seek the One that had breathed the breath of life into me. Thus, I sought the Creator of Heaven and Earth and everything in it. I prayed and cried and cried and prayed. I begged and pleaded and pleaded and begged. God was so attentive and responsive when I first became **saved** and now it appeared that He was not answering me again. I was getting extremely frustrated. My heart was heavy, my soul was burdened, and my emotions were sporadically all over the place. I needed to hear from God and the Silence was not sitting well with me. As difficult as the silence was, it was just as difficult to come face to face with the possibility of death. The doctor told me that the tumor was so deeply embedded in my breast that the biopsy needle could not reach it; hence, I would have to have surgery which was one of my biggest fears.

My first surgery determined the diagnosis of the unreachable tissue. The results rendered that the tumor was cancerous because it had jagged edges which meant malignant, as opposed to the smooth edges which meant benign. The diagnosis of the unreachable tissue had me deeply agitated. I knew they had to provide a diagnosis, but I did not want to hear this—not today—not now—not ever!

The second surgery not only consisted of extracting the malignant tumor, but it included the insertion of an access port where the chemotherapy (chemo) would be administered. The surgeon commented:

> "I will go outside of the perimeter of the tumor to ensure
> that I get it all."

I am sure the surgeon's statement was meant to comfort me, but it only increased unwanted anxiety. I thought to myself: of course, you will get it all; is there another option? I think not! Why is this even a consideration? Of course, you will annihilate the malignant cancer. Of course, you will utterly destroy the unwanted invasion. Of course, you will obliterate the opponent forever. I needed this to be a mistake. I needed the doctor's office to call and say, I am sorry, we misread the report and you are fine. That did not happen. I became truly petrified. I knew with absolute certainty that I was entering the fight of my life.

I had no energy to fight. I just wanted this situation to disappear. I felt saddened and alone. "God, where are you?" Silence! "I need to hear from You, God, but You are not answering me and I do not understand why?" I cried out, "God, are you hearing me?" Silence. "I need to hear from You God, but you are not answering." The quietness was playing havoc on my mind. I could not understand nor grasp God's unresponsiveness. I was trying to stay positive and to stand on the *Word of God* but even that became an absolute struggle. The struggle felt like a tug-of-war, one moment I was trusting God, and the next moment I was wavering. I shouted at the top of my lungs, "God, I need you to take this illness away from me! Are you listening, God?" Silence! Again, I shouted, "I need to hear from You God, please answer!" This apparent abandonment crushed my spirit. Fear was building up in me. The fear kept filling my mind with what-ifs. I begged God to remove this fear from me. I begged and begged and begged until I could not beg anymore. Yet, all I got was His silence!

I felt hopeless and weak and I did not feel that I had the strength to endure this journey. I was frightened to death to go through another surgery, let alone chemotherapy. I closed my eyes and cried until I could not cry anymore. I wanted this situation to be gone and I wanted it to be gone now. Instead, fear came and sat right down beside me again and would not move. God had spoken to me before through *His Word* in Proverbs 3:5–6 and Isaiah 41:10—but now, I was not hearing anything but silence! Lord, I need a Word I said, yet all I continue to get is His silence! I know people say:

"Silence is Golden"

But this is the one time that I needed silence to take on a voice of its own and answer me! God was the One who was silent and I did not know why He would not answer me. The deafening silence was blaring in my heart.

Hello?
God?
God, can you hear me?
God, where are You?

I sighed and allowed the tears to flow like a rushing river bursting through a broken dam. I was that broken dam and I was a mess. Just the thought of having been confirmed that I have cancer had filled me with an unbelievable amount of frustration, worry, and anxiety.

One day at work I had a conversation with a guy who had had a miraculous healing. This guy shared with me that his doctor diagnosed him with terminal cancer and they gave him a few months to live. He decided that since he had a scheduled appointment with death; he was going to live out his last days enjoying life to the fullest. He did not want anything including family standing in his way of living out his last days. He decided to leave his family (wife and kids) to fully enjoy the last days before his expiration date. He was so upset with God and he told Him as much. He lifted his head to the sky and said:

"If You say You are God then heal me."

He made the statement, left his family, and went on his mission to live out his supposedly last days. Then one day, it dawned on him that it was five years later, and he was still alive. He went back to the doctors, got another X-ray and nothing was there. He showed them the X-ray that he had kept. They confirmed that there was a mass on his past X-ray, however; his current X-ray was clean and there was no mass present. Then he remembered the words that he spoke to God.

He became overwhelmed with gratefulness. He turned his life around and turned back to God. Mercifully, God restored the family. He had realized that God had performed a supernatural healing. He told me that if God healed him supernaturally, then He could heal me in the same manner. His love and trust in God were very evident. I wanted to believe just the way he did, but I was not certain if I had the same faith to believe in a supernatural healing for myself. The touching story of his supernatural healing had lifted my spirits and gave me hope.

Although I was intrigued with his supernatural healing, I was still perplexed on what treatment method I would consider. I continuously spoke to God about what avenue to walk, but I did not feel like I had an answer from God. I poured my heart out to God and relentlessly asked Him over and over which treatment method should I take? I had no idea how long He was going to take to answer but I pleaded with Him to please answer me soon. I needed to make a decision whether to go holistic, take the chemotherapy, or believe in the supernatural. Time was ticking and I had no idea what to do. I heard powerful testimonies on all sides of the triangle (holistic, chemotherapy, supernatural), which made the decision that much harder.

Even though it seemed as if God was not hearing me, I did not stop crying out to Him. I was talking to God about what to do as far as my treatments were concerned. In the middle of our conversation, the phone rang. I was not sure if I should answer it or let it go to voice mail since I was talking with God. I decided to answer the phone. My girlfriend Anelia, a dear sweet long-time friend just happened to be calling. We only converse on the phone about two times a year, however; our calls last forever because we play catch-up. I truly thank God for putting her into my life because she has been a good friend and a precious blessing to me. As we conversed, I struggled with whether or not to share this information with her for fear of what her response may be. I decided to share my situation of being diagnosed with breast cancer. And before I could comment further, she interrupted me, and the first words out of her mouth were:

> **"Lisa, Lisa, whatever you do, take the chemo.**
> My girlfriend is dying because she would not undergo chemotherapy. She took the holistic approach. My mom took chemo, and she is alive."

I accepted this as an answer from God especially since I was just in a conversation with Him. I was gratefully thankful because God had heard my cry and answered my prayer. God's timely response gave me a glimmer of hope—that peacefully quieted my mind. God's grace has no limitation and He can heal anyone, anytime, at any moment, on any day. I know that whatever route anyone takes the person must not waver! The grace of God knew I was a newbie Christian and I would waver. God is not limited, and He can heal in any format, whether it is holistic, chemotherapy, or supernatural. My healing came through chemotherapy via the grace of God, yet someone else's may come in one of the other ways—there is no one way to be healed. And for that I thank God!

On the day of my surgery, a nun asked if she could pray with me. I agreed and she affirmed my request to God. She said:

> "There are angels all around you."

That alone touched my soul since my request to God before the surgery was, "Lord, please put angels all around me." After the surgery, the surgeon informed me that the tumor and some lymph nodes were removed. The surgeon shared that specific details would be forthcoming from my assigned Oncologist.

The day I met my assigned Oncologist was something I will never forget. I was escorted to a cold drably hospital room. The Oncologist entered the room on his cellphone and carried a conversation in front of me as if I was not there. He did not wash his hands, but came in and sat down in front of me while still talking on his cellphone. When he finally ended the call, he introduced himself and told me that he would be my doctor. He told me that my cancer was aggressive, but I could probably live about five years or maybe a little longer with the treatments. He informed me that I would be taking chemotherapy which consisted of three drugs Adriamycin, Cytoxan, and Taxol; which is also known as "ACT." The doctor was doom and gloom, and depressing. I nor my mom cared for his bedside manner. His matter-of-fact statement of death was very disheartening. That death sentence that he affirmed began to wreak havoc on my mind. I left his office feeling completely defeated.

I knew I had to go into prayer about this Oncologist and what he was saying. And to prayer, I went! I did not want to die, yet it seemed in five years or so, my fate would be sealed. I was never so scared in my life. I cried out to God to give me a different Oncologist. I did not want this Oncologist. I was told that the Oncologist who I desired was unavailable because there was no room in the inn (the chemotherapy clinic was full). They had no vacant beds (reclining chairs) available for me in that particular Oncologist Clinic.

I appeal to the Oncologist who had no available rooms and I poured out my heart to her. I asked her to please take me or recommend someone else because the assigned Oncologist had me completely stressed out. I explained to her what had happened, and she said:

> "During this time, it is important that you remain stress-free as possible. I would take you myself, but there is no space available at this clinic. If you can go to my other clinic then I will be your Oncologist."

I had never felt so much relief after her statement. It was like a weight was lifted off my shoulders. I was ever so grateful that God had made a way where there appeared to be no way. The other clinic was about an hour or so away. I would have driven to Timbuktu to get away from the first Oncologist. I could not stop thanking God. I knew without a doubt that God heard my desperate plea and for that, I was truly grateful. God had shown up for me again and I could not stop thanking Him.

We (my mom and I) drove to the other clinic to see where the building was located and to visit the chemotherapy suite. When we got there, we were told we needed to have made an appointment prior and that we could not just show up to take a tour. My mom was explaining that we had driven over an hour to get here . . . and while they were talking, I mentally checked out of that conversation and I went straight into prayer again. I found myself doing a lot of this lately. Before I could ask God for favor, a nurse from the chemo suite who had just happened to be passing by overheard our conversation and overridden the denial from the receptionist and permitted us into the chemo suite. The nurse personally gave us the tour. I love how God always knows what we need before we ask. God's Word affirms this in Scripture: *I will answer them before they even call to me. While they are still talking about their needs, I will go ahead and answer their prayers—Isaiah 65:24 (NLT)*

As if that was not enough, God in His loving-kindness blessed me with a vision while driving down a winding back road on my way home from work. The awesomeness of the vision blew my mind. A big picture flashed in front of me. It was like watching a movie. The vision was so clear that I instinctively had a knowing of what I was seeing. I likened this to Daniel 10:1 (ESV) that says: *And he understood the word and had an understanding of the vision.* It was not a daydream or a thought but a literal vision. It touched my heart that God would take the time to show me—next steps. I could not wait to get home to draw what I saw and write down what it meant.

The vision was comprised of three circles. There was a small poisonous bubbly circle (chemotherapy drug—Adriamycin); inside of a bigger less poisonous bubbly circle (chemotherapy drug—Cytoxan); and around the entire perimeter was a clear, calm circle. I instantly knew that the clear calm circle was the grace of God. I had a conversation with God because what the first Oncologists told me did not match the vision that God had just given to me. In my vision, I saw two medications and

God's grace around the two medications—not three medications. The first Oncologist told me that they would administer three medications (ACT—Adriamycin, Cytoxan, Taxol) simultaneously. As I mull over this, I began to wonder if I had deciphered the vision incorrectly.

When the second Oncologist took me under her wing, she began to inform me of the various treatment options. She said that she would like for me to consider a new method. The new method would be to administer only two drugs first (AC) and then (T) would follow. I got so excited because that matched the vision that God had shown me which was two drugs not three. The Oncologist continued explaining why this method was my best option. I had already made up my mind, but I continued to listen. She stated that:

> "This type of treatment has worked well with other patients with the same aggressive cancer."

She also informed me of the side effects which was paralysis in the hands and feet. I did not care about that because I was focusing on what I saw from the vision that God provided. Although this treatment was fairly new at the time when I took it (2006), it is now a common practice with people who have aggressive cancers per my research. I was immediately relieved because this was exactly what was revealed to me. I saw two poisonous drugs that were to be given to me simultaneously along with God's grace surrounding the entire process. I could not hold back my optimism. God had shown me how I was going to be healed and I believed Him.

The chemotherapy began in the *Summer*. The chemo suite was filled with patients of all ages, except children. I found out that chemotherapy actually had a nickname at the hospital. Its nickname was red liquid fire. Basically, because it is a red liquid and kills everything in its path—good and bad cells. The nurses tried to make light of the situation to keep the atmosphere pleasant and filled with hope. The staff was super supportive and very accommodating to everyone.

The chemotherapy was administered through a port access placed in my chest during the second surgery. Many people opted for the chemo port access in order to alleviate direct injections via the veins. However, this lady whose chair was beside mine did not have a port. She allowed them to use her veins and she had sores and awful scarring from the chemo injections. The nurses were having a hard time getting the IV (Intravenous) into her arm. She was annoyed, the nurses were annoyed, and they called even more nurses to assist who were also unsuccessful and annoyed. I began to pray and ask God to please help the nurses to get the IV into her arm. Wahla! Can you believe it? Just like the snap of fingers! He answered my prayer for the lady beside me. That touched my heart in a big way. I realized at that very moment that God is a very caring God and a very loving God. I immediately thanked God for this beautiful instantaneous wondrous blessing for my chemo suite-mate beside me who was having a rough time.

Chemotherapy took a toll on my entire body. I was extremely sick. I was constantly vomiting and all I wanted to do after the infusion was to sleep. I could not wait to get home and into my bed. I could not eat nor did I have an appetite. There was an awful disgusting taste in my mouth that just lingered. No matter what I ate, nothing would stay down. After every treatment, I would dry heave and that was hard and extremely painful. By the third day, I would feel somewhat better and the heaving would curtail.

My bed became my refuge and a place of peace as long as I could sleep. However, as I mentioned, on the first two days I would be running to the bathroom spewing out contents. I could not eat nor did I have an appetite. One day I jumped up running to the bathroom because I felt the vomit frenzy about to attack. The heaving made me choke, cough, and turn my face deep red. I could not get this vomiting frenzy under control. My throat was raw and on fire. I cried out to God as I hugged the toilet and told Him that I could not take this anymore and I asked Him to please stop this vomiting. By the sheer grace of God, the vomiting immediately ceased. I got up slowly from hugging the toilet, I simply said, "Lord, I just want to be held." I leaned against the bathroom wall and closed my eyes. I do not know how long I was there, but I know I was in His arms because someone was holding me. I cannot begin to explain how this embrace made me feel. There is nothing like being in the arms of God and I did not want Him to let me go. This only happened to me once, but it was an unforgettable experience that is permanently etched upon my heart. I knew then that He heard my heartfelt cry. I never vomited another day from that point forward. I was still very sick, but I never vomited again. Only God can rescue you in a time of desperate need. To say I was thankful would be an understatement. I know what I felt. I know He is real. I know He held me. I know a miracle when I see it because He had just performed another one again!

My mom stayed with me the first two days and took care of me and my kids. She had to get back home to my dad who also had cancer. I did not fully realize all that was on my mother's plate. She took such excellent care of me during this *Season*. I could never thank her enough for being there for me. Nor could I thank my dad enough for releasing her without making her feel guilty. The truth is—we both needed her.

Upon my routine scheduled appointment at the chemo suite, I was told that my chemo port looked to be infected. Only five percent of cases have infected chemo ports and I somehow became a part of that statistic. They prescribed some medication for me and told me if the infection does not heal, in which most cases they do not (as the nurse communicated this to me), then they would not be able to administer the chemotherapy upon my next visit and another surgery would have to be scheduled to insert a new chemo port. The other alternative was to take the chemotherapy intravenously and after what I witnessed with one of my chemo suite-mates—that was not going to happen. I began to do what I did best in this *Season,* cry, plea, and pray. I asked God to heal the infected port so that I would not have to have another surgery.

The doctor prescribed an ointment that I would need to apply until my next scheduled visit. I looked at the pus that oozed from the chemo port and decided to speak over it. I remembered the **Bible** said to speak those things that are not as they are (see Romans 4:17). As I applied

the ointment, I would say, "I am healed and what I see is a healing pus."
I told myself: "self, this is what we are going to say and believe. Every
time I see the pus, I am going to call it healing pus"—and I did just that.

Upon my return to the chemo suite, they checked my port and was
amazed at the healing results. The nurse commented that:

> "It does not look as if you had an infection. I have never
> seen an infected port healed."

But God! I knew once again that only the *Hand of God* could have
done this. This would be my first lesson of speaking those things
that I wanted to see *(calleth those things which be not* as *though they were*
(Romans 4:17—KJV)). Each miraculous act drew me closer to God. I
thank God for being attentive to my cries while listening to my prayers.
In the 2 Kings 20:5 (NIV), God told Hezekiah: *I have heard your prayer
and seen your tears; I will heal you.* Like God healed Hezekiah, He
listened to my cries, please, and prayers and healed my infected port. I
was so grateful to not have to undergo another surgery. God's hand was
with me and because of that, I had a tremendous sense of peace even
amid this horrifying storm brewing.

In the chemo suite, it would take hours for the chemotherapy to be
infused throughout my body. There were numerous reading materials
such as magazines, books, etc., but I only had a taste for the *Word of
God*. I only read the **Bible** for the entire duration of the chemotherapy
treatments. I only wanted to talk with God and that was it. I stayed
very close to Him during this travailing *Season*. I had the foresight and
an inkling of wisdom to know that I could not do this without God.
I had no idea how the cards would be dealt, nor how my hand would
be played. Yet, I believe without a doubt that God was my only hope!

The one thing that I could not shake was—why. I asked God over
and over and over again—why? Why God? Why? I was not running
from Him anymore, I simply wanted to know why. I believed in Him,

but I could not calculate the "why-factor." I wanted to make sense of this situation, but I could not. The constant question that bothered me was—why me? Then God sent me an angel (Adriana) who listened to my heartfelt cry and she simply looked at me with love and said:

"Why not you?"

I never thought about it like that. This is not what I expected to hear from this beautiful *Woman of God*. I could not even get upset with her because she said it with no mal intent. She shared Scriptures that spoke exactly to my ordeal. The Scripture she shared was 1 Peter 4:12 (NIV): *Dear friends, do not be surprised at the fiery ordeal that has come on you to test you, as though something strange was happening to you.* This led me to seek other Scriptures that talk about plights and I came across James 1:12 (NIV): *Blessed is the one who perseveres under trial because, having stood the test, that person will receive the crown of life that the LORD has promised to those who love him."* And again, in John 16:33 (HCSB): *You will have suffering in this world. Be courageous! I have conquered the world."* And lastly, 1 Peter 5:9 (NLT): *Remember that your family of believers all over the world is going through the same kind of suffering you are.* These Scriptures moved me to look from a godly perspective. The more I peered from a godly perspective, the more the eyes of my heart were open to the understandings of God.

I remember God's Word telling me not to be dismayed or afraid (see Isaiah 41:10) and how He brought peace (see Philippians 4:7) to my life amid this fierce tsunami crashing down upon all around me. Witnessing the *Word of God* working in my life had put me in a different mindset. I began to search the **Bible** for healing Scriptures. I searched the Scriptures that spoke to my current circumstances. I listed them out and believed that these Scriptures were medicinal and the best treatment that I could ever take. I would say these Scriptures three times a day in the name of the Father, Son, and Holy Spirit. I would say the Scriptures every morning, without fail!

One of the Scriptures I landed upon was Revelation 22:2 (MSG) which says: *The Tree of Life was planted on each side of the river, producing twelve kinds of fruit, a ripe fruit each month. The leaves of the Tree are for healing the nations.* I believed that God's Word was the key to my healing. I sought twenty-four Scriptures and I hung on those precious nuggets for my healing. I knew that there was life in the *Word of God*, and I believed that that life would bring sweet medicinal healing. The Tree of Life is what I feasted upon during this entire *Season*.

TREE OF LIFE

The leaves of the Tree are for healing the nations.
Revelation 22:2 (MSG)

24 FRUIT TREES
Tree of Life was planted on each side of the river

Almond: *1st Peter 2:24*	**Mango:** *Mark 5:34*
Apple: *2 Kings 20:5*	**Mulberry:** *Matthew 4:23*
Apricot: *Exodus 15:26*	**Olive:** *Matthew 8:7*
Avocado: *Exodus 23:25*	**Orange:** *Matthew 9:35*
Banana: *Jeremiah 17:14*	**Papaya:** *Proverbs 17:22*
Cacao: *Jeremiah 30:17*	**Peach:** *Psalms 6:2*
Cherry: *Jeremiah 33:6*	**Pear:** Psalms 30:2
Coconut: *Isaiah 38:16*	**Pineapple:** *Psalms 41:3*

Fig: Isaiah *53:3–5*	**Plantain:** *Psalms 103:3*
Kiwi: *Luke 5:17*	**Plum:** *Psalms 107:20*
Kumquat: *Luke 8:50*	**Plum:** *Psalms 118:17*
Lemon: *Luke 13:12*	**Pomegranate:** *Psalms 147:3*

The Tree of life was planted on each side of the river. I took twelve fruits (Scriptures) from one side and twelve fruits from the other side—equaling twenty-four fruits. I fed myself three times daily. I also coupled the prayers of Impossible (see below). Knowing that nothing was impossible for God meant a lot to me in this *Season*. I had witnessed many miraculous signs and wonders on this journey. This journey was teaching me to put my complete trust in God.

- Genesis 18:14 (GW): *Is anything too hard for the Lord?*
- Matthew 19:26 (NIV): *But with God all things are possible for God.*
- Mark 9:23 (GW): *Everything is possible for the person who believes.*
- Mark 10:27 (KJV): *For with God, all things are possible.*
- Job 42:2 (ESV): *I know that you can do all things, and that no purpose of yours can be thwarted.*

PRAYER

Lord, I believe that Your healing is available to me. I thank You for these Healing Scriptures that are a medicinal balm to my heart, mind, body, and soul. I thank You for teaching me how to hide these precious Scriptures deep into the depths of my soul. I thank You for teaching me how to take them faithfully three times a day in the name of the Father, Son, and Holy Spirit, the beautiful Trinity of blessings. *I do believe; help my unbelief (Mark 9:24—CSB).*

Everything has a divine plan and purpose even when you do not understand the plan. We plan, God plans, and clearly, His plan is without question the best—

"He just does not feel the need to check in with you."

I heard this commentary on television and it spoke to me so clearly. The Omnipotent planner's plan is nothing less than perfection. No matter what is going on in your life currently, God says it like this: *For I know the plans I have for you, "declares the Lord," plans to prosper you and not to harm you, plans to give you hope and a future—Jeremiah 29:11(NIV).* I knew that I could not do anything on my own and the **Bible** affirms this: *Humanly speaking, it is impossible. But with God everything is possible (Matthew 19:26 NLT).* The hardest part is standing still and trusting that God has your best interest at heart. Believing in the unseen is the believer's guide to faith. Corrie ten Boom says it like this:

> *"Faith sees the invisible, believes the unbelievable, and receives the impossible."*

Logic cannot produce faith, only your belief can. In Hebrews 11:6 (NIV), the **Bible** says that: *And without faith, it is impossible to please God, because anyone who comes to him must believe that he exists and that he rewards those who earnestly seek him.* My sincere heartfelt desire is to press earnestly towards seeking Him.

ALERT: God had answered me on many occasions, but it was not the answer that I was seeking. I wanted Him to remove the diagnosis. He is God, so He could do this if He so desired, yet He chose not to! Answers from God will come, whether it is yes, no, or wait; an answer is certain to come. We may not like the answer, but we can be sure that His answer is for certain the best even when the request goes unanswered, it is still an answer. Lord, I prayed: "help me with my belief-o-meter, trust-o-meter, faith-o-meter, and especially the wait-o-meter as I put my trust completely in You—even Your unanswered prayers."

The sun is shining from the light of the Son. It is a
bright beautiful day, not a cloud is in sight.

───◦∞◦───

*Faith walks on the path of belief by the rivers where the stones of hope,
trust, and peace are nestled alongside the sands by the seashores.*

Unsung Season

THE PRAISE

One beautiful Sunday morning, I attended a church in Washington, D.C. Upon entering the church, I noticed some unknown words hanging from an intricately designed fabric. The beautiful fabric all began with the name of Jehovah. I knew the name Jehovah but not the words following Jehovah's name. After the service, I went back to peer at the names on the beautiful intrinsic fabric. I wondered what each of these names meant. The names drew me in as the air one breathes. The names took a hold of me and thus went pen to paper:

1. Jehovah Jireh
2. Jehovah Nissi
3. Jehovah Rapha
4. Jehovah Rohi
5. Jehovah Shalom
6. Jehovah Shammah
7. Jehovah Tsidkenu

When I got home, I looked up the names that I saw on the beautiful exquisite fabric. I found out that these were the names of God. I had never heard of these names before that day. I wrote the meanings down and pondered over the seven names of God. I wondered how many more names of God there were. I started with Jehovah who I knew was a name of God, but I never considered whether Jehovah meant what I thought it meant. This opened up a whole new world for me. For some people, this may appear trivial, but for me, it was an eye-opener that would lead me to seek and search for even more names of God.

As I was searching each of the names of God, I realized that each name was attached to a Scripture. Now, hold on a minute, I know what some of you are thinking, but remember I am a newbie, so let me tell my story for those of you who just went duh! Everything about coming into the Kingdom was nothing less than amazing to me. It was like I had fresh new eyes that kept making fresh new discoveries. Old to some—but new and relevant to me.

I used the New King James Version of the **Bible** to find the Scriptures which related to the names of God. There were many results on the names of God. I looked up JEHOVAH (Exodus 6:2–3) which meant *The Lord*. I also realized that many Scriptures referenced and pointed to the names of God, but for this story, I am choosing to only use one Scripture. I have written the names of God in alphabetical order; however, this is not the order in which I initially saw the names.

One of the first names discovered was JEHOVAH JIREH (Genesis 22:14); The-Lord-Will-Provide. The second Name in alphabetical order was JEHOVAH NISSI (Exodus 17:15–16); *The-Lord-Is-My-Banner*. The third in sequential order was JEHOVAH RAPHA (Exodus 15:26); *I am the LORD who heals you*. The fourth in succession was JEHOVA ROHI (Psalms 23:1); *The Lord is my shepherd*. The fifth in the series was JEHOVAH SHALOM (Judges 6:24); *The-Lord-Is-Peace*. The sixth in the pecking structure was JEHOVAH SHAMMAH (Ezekiel 48:35); *THE LORD IS THERE*. The seventh trailing in the progression of names of God was JEHOVAH TSIDKENU (Jeremiah 23:6); THE LORD OUR RIGHTEOUSNESS.

I had to do some research and study because when I first wrote the names of God down, there was no instant interpretation of what I was writing down. In my research, I learned that many of these names have various spellings like Rapha is also Rophe, and Rohi is also Raah; to name a few. The spelling was based on whether it was Hebrew, Greek, or Aramaic. What was pertinent to me was the meaning. As I continued to search the names of God a song was birthed in my spirit. The structure of the first part of the song was based on rhyming. And the structure of the second part of the song was based on sounding. Sounding is when you make words rhymes through a rhythmic flow:

- Jehovah Jireh
- Jehovah Nissi
- Jehovah Rapha
- Jehovah Rohi
  - *First Stanza*
- Jehovah Shammah
- Jehovah Tsidkenu
- Jehovah Shalom
  - *Second Stanza*

God inspired me to write a song. The song was titled "Thank You" and spoke to who God is. I had no idea how to make the second stanza flow and I told God that. I also suggested that He give me another name because seven is an uneven number and eight would be better. I amazed myself at times, at how I wanted to direct God. But God, in His loving patience and mercy did it His way, as it should be done. Although I preferred to have eight rhyming names, God made it work with seven names. Seven is the number of completion and He had completed the song. Watching the hand of God in wonderment kept me constantly amazed.

This was the foundational birthing of the song that God put into my spirit. It had to be God because writing music was not my thing nor was it something that I had ever considered. With God, I composed a song from these names. Initially, the song was titled "Jehovah." And as the lyrics evolved, I felt prompted to change the title to "Thank You." How glorious is it to thank the LORD of the universe who showers upon us in ways we can never imagine? I thanked God repeatedly for this hidden treasure that was given to me after I got **saved**. I copyrighted the song on May 13, 2005.

As I mentioned before, writing and composing music was never a forethought, not on my agenda, not a desire, not a concept, nor was it something that I had ever considered. I asked myself where did this desire to write music come from? This spiritual blessing of a lyrical song and music came after I surrendered my life to Christ. Coincidence? I do not think so. Now, let's be clear about this. I cannot sing (as I have been told by many). I cannot play an instrument. I cannot play music by ear. I cannot read or write musical notes. I never thought to write a song, yet the lyrics and music flowed through me like a professional composer. It was as if the music was my natural gifting. Let me also add that I took a Spiritual Gifting test twice and musical composition nor anything related to music was populated as my gift. Yet, God knew I loved music and He used the music to minister to my spirit. GOD can extract anything out of nothing (*no talent*) and take nothing and turn it into something (*uncut raw talent out of nowhere*). God did just that—when He blessed me with a song that appeared out of nowhere. I loved to sing and I loved to sing the song that God had graciously blessed me to compose.

I am the person you see in the grocery store, walking down the aisle singing aloud to whatever song is coming from the store speakers. I truly enjoy singing! I had tried to share my song with some friends who laughed at me; thus, I thought better not to ever do that again. The importance of me sharing this gifting is to touch on the awesomeness of God. The interesting part is when I sing it; I hear the music playing in the background along with voices. As I sing the song, I revel in the glory of God and how the song speaks directly to me. Again, it still astounds me that He blessed me with something out of nothing. Nothing, *N*othing, no music experience whatsoever, yet He gave me a song musically based and that blessed me tremendously. In addition to the song that God had helped me to compose; He provided me with a Scripture to accompany the song:

> The LORD is my strength and my shield; my heart trusts
> in Him, and I am helped.

Therefore my heart rejoices, and I give thanks to Him with my song (Psalm 28:7—BSB).

This particular Scripture prompted me to change the title from "Jehovah" to "Thank You." The very last line spoke volumes to me. I have echoed my sentiments of thanks to Him on a continuum basis for everything, every day, and in every way. The awe-inspiring wonders of God in this *Season* were simply amazing. My heart was exploding with thanks and praise.

I sincerely wanted to connect with the heart of God. I prayed a prayer frequently asking God to touch my heart so that my heart would be aligned with His heart. The song gives thanks to God. And if I had to summarize the song, it would read like this:

> I thank you Heavenly Father for being my provider when I could not provide for myself. I thank you, God, for being my battle-fighter when I had no strength to fight. I thank you precious Father for being my Healer. It was not the way I wanted to be healed, yet you loved me enough to confirm that I would be healed. I thank you Glorious Father for being my Shepherd. I was the lost sheep. Your love, as My Shepherd chased me down and loved me back into the sheep pen. You brought me back into the family as I entered through the sheep gate. I know there was nothing about me that was right. But when I accepted you, I became the righteousness of You (God). Although chaos, doubt, and fear kept poking their ugly head up and taunting me; You would simply point me in the direction of *Your Word* that gives me: *Peace . . . that surpasses all understanding (Philippians 4:7—ESV).*

God had given me another song during this *Season*. Just like the first song, the original title was also changed. Initially, the second song was "Can't Find My Way" and it ended up becoming "Trust." One day I was in the shower thinking about the two songs that God had given to me. So, I asked Him, "why did You give me these songs?" And the answer came to me as clear as day,

"Because you needed them at the time."

So, I began to sing the songs while listening intently to the lyrics. I considered every word carefully. It was like my life was unfolding as I sang the songs. The revelation of each lyric was made vividly clear. I think I poured out more tears than what was coming out of the showerhead. I was in such a state of grateful praise that I could not stop thanking God. It was nothing short of amazing that God knew exactly what I needed and exactly when I needed it. God is amazingly awesome even though we overlook His bountiful blessings daily. I sat and considered His amazement in my heart:

- Isn't it amazing that God blesses us bountifully, yet we cannot see what is right before our eyes?
- Isn't it amazing that we chase everything meaningless, yet we avoid a meaningful God?
- Isn't it amazing that we look for love in all the wrong places, yet we dismiss the love of God?
- Isn't it amazing that we will read literature about God, yet we won't read the **Bible,** the actual *Word of God*?
- Isn't it amazing that we will shout at the top of our lungs for a celebrity, yet we dumb down our voice and posture in the *House of God*?
- Isn't it amazing that we will get up to go to work, yet we will not get up to pray?
- Isn't it amazing that you can have something at your fingertips and not even know it?

God is at the fingertips of our hearts waiting to have a relationship with us and many times we just brush Him off to the side while we miss every blessing that He has for us. I was learning to tug on the heartstrings of God's love. The heartstrings of His love came through the vehicle called music. God knew I love music and our relationship grew from this venue. Learning to trust God would be my daily walk and thanking God would become my daily posture—after all these were the two takeaways from the songs that He had given to me, trusting Him and being thankful.

On my walk towards God, the two most important life lessons I was learning were to lean into God and to develop a relationship with Him. God is Omnipresent. He is always there and always available. At times it can seem that He has moved far from us, but the reality is that we have moved far from Him. God is the same today, yesterday, and will be tomorrow and forever. He has not moved. We simply do not know His voice. His voice is found in *His Word*. We have to lean in to capture the essence of His heart to hear His powerful Word in His power-filled book, the **Bible**. The Scripture says it like this: But s*eek Ye first the Kingdom of God, and His righteousness, and all these things shall be added onto you* (Matthew 6:33—KJV). As I began wholeheartedly seeking God, various things began to unfold in my life—good, bad, beautiful, and ugly. I would eventually learn that all these things would make me a better individual. The Scripture says it like this: *And, we know that God causes everything to work together for the good of those who love God and are called according to his purpose for them (Romans 8:28—NLT).*

I continued to seek God and press no matter how I felt, no matter what things looked like, and no matter what people said. I purposely pressed to be in the presence of God because that is where I could find my ultimate peace. As I continued to seek God, He was revealing much through *His Word*. I believed *His Word* and I was learning to trust His guidance. I truly believed that there was nothing that He could not do. In this *Season* of my life, believing was not an option but a choice. I chose to believe amid my current fiery storm brewing (chemotherapy). The battle was lengthy and very toilsome, yet the grace of God kept me. Because of His loving-kindness and compassion, He chose to give me two songs. I sang these two songs over and over and over again. They meant so much to me because the songs spoke to everything I was experiencing during this harsh *Season* of my life. Just like He gave me a Scripture to go with the first song titled "Thank You;" He gave me the following Scripture to go with the second song titled "Trust:"

- Psalms 55:23 (NIV): *But as for me, I **trust** in You.*

The second song, "Trust" is about individual seeking answers from anyone who would listen to the cries of her plea. The problem is the individual is seeking the answer from everyone else except God. When I wrote the song, God had provided the answer in which I was searching. I cannot tell you how many times I would question God and try and understand why my life was the way it was—SMH (shaking my head). The answer was right in front of me; after all, I wrote it down. Had I truly taken the lyrics into my heart; I would have understood what I had written. No one could truly help my broken aching soul but God. In this song, God wanted me to come to Him first and foremost so that I would lean into Him and harness His Trust.

To harness His trust, I would need to seek Him first. The more I sought the Lord, the more God revealed Himself to me. And the more God revealed Himself to me; the more I fell in love with Jesus. Jesus became my **Unsung Hero.** When I looked up the word **unsung** it referred to a person who has done great feats and is given little or no praise or recognition. Jesus fits that particular mold in my life. He had done so much for me, yet I took it all for granted. The songs He gave to me were just one of His beautiful giftings. Both songs spoke to every area of my life. He was teaching me to be in a posture of thankfulness and to fully trust in Him—no matter what! My heart is touched every time I sing the songs that God has blessed me with. And when I sing the songs, it is like He is watering my heart with His love and refreshing my soul with a peaceful healing balm through His Word.

=============================== **FORECAST** ===============================

Clear blue skies with a high of 50 degrees. It is a beautiful *Spring* morning, birds chirping, bees buzzing and flowers are budding.

———— ∞ ————

One-touch from God leads me beside quiet waters and refreshes my soul like sweet dewdrops in the pasturelands of Thanks and Trust!

6

Unusual Season

THE PROMPTING

"No! No! No!" I shouted. "No! No! No!" I shouted even louder as if it would make a difference. I instinctively knew the reality of my situation. I had no control over the circumstance. I was helpless and the one who could help me was the one controlling the situation. I was frightened. No, I was scared to death! I began to panic! I could sense the intensity all around me. I could not find my breath. I could not stop nor control what was happening to me. This devastating force that was upon me was relentless and was not willing to release me. I pleaded for mercy but all I got was a tightening grip around my signature ponytail.

Whack! "No," I cried out. My signature ponytail had just been lopped off. I stared at the hair in my hand with utter disbelief. The incredulous force began lifting me by the remaining hair in my scrunchie ponytail holder. I went limp like a ragdoll being handled by a disappointed doll-maker. I was completely drained of all of my physical strength. With great sorrow and a heavy heart, I asked myself: "why is this happening to me?" But, ironically enough, I already knew as the inquiring words cascaded from my lips. Yes, sadly, I knew exactly why this was happening to me. Time was not on my side. My life was vanishing right before my eyes. I became deeply overwhelmed with remorse. I let go and completely surrendered my entire being to this massive force and . . .

I woke up from a deep surreal sleep or did I escape from a knowing fate? I could not help but wonder, was this a dream or a divine message? I reflected on the scene where I was lifted by my hair and I thought about the Scripture in Ezekiel: *He stretched out what looked like a hand and took me by the hair of my head*—Ezekiel 8:3 (NIV). Again, I could not help but wonder if my life was ending? Was my number being called? Did I get another chance? I deeply pondered these eerie feelings. The more I pondered, the more concern swept over me. I contemplated the vastness of this nightmarish dream. I wondered, where do dreams come from? Do they bring a message to heed or are they based on what you last experienced, watched on television, thought, or even worried about?

Looking back, my dreams seem to be my nighttime foe. Every night I dreamt without fail. I did not always remember my dreams, except for the horrid ones because I was always jolted upright out of my sleep. When this happened, I would not want to go back to sleep. I would get up and start doing something to distract me from the nightmare. The reason that I would not go back to sleep is that the horrid dream would always pick up where it left off. Thus, for years, I hated going to sleep. I used to envy people who say they do not dream. I truly wished that this could be my story. There have been too many times when sleep would evade me because I was scared of what night terrors would await me. My house was the beacon for the neighborhood. There was a light on in every room including the bathroom. I could never get a good night's sleep even with the lights on. I was so scared of my frightening dreams that sweet undisturbed sleep alluded me for years.

I began to seek God concerning these tormented dreams and how to deal with this fear. I love the uniqueness in how God provides answers. One day He put an angelic messenger on my path who I did not know and we somehow ended up on the topic of dreams. I shared my angst concerning my nightmares. The angelic messenger simply said:

"Stop running from your nightmares. If you want to defeat them, you will have to face them."

That was the last thing that I wanted to hear, yet it was exactly what I needed to heed. I decided to test the hypothesis for its veracity. As on cue, the nightmare returned as if it was sitting there waiting on me to shut my eyes and go to sleep. It's amazing what you can remember while you are asleep. I remembered what the angelic messenger had spoken to me. This time I did not panic. I refused to run. I stood bold and looked at the nightmare from a different perspective. I faced the monstrosity, acknowledge the nightmare, and brought it to God. I asked God to show me what I needed to glean from this unsettling dream. The nightmares did not dissipate instantaneously, but the atrocity of the fear took a quick nose-dive and began dwindling; simply because I trusted God to deliver me from my fears. What I learned is that fear cannot stand in the face of God. It is okay to recognize fear, but it is not okay to allow fear to be in control. When we allow fear to be in control, we create a self-made prison. God provided the keys to unlock my self-made prison and I opened the door and set myself free.

ALERT: Don't allow the pressure of stress to put you in a bubble of fear. Fear is a debilitating evil that will hold you back from your true destiny, even the destination of sweet sleep. Your nightmare, the frigid cold dream may be your night-aware trying to bring you a message.

Once again, I was shaken from a nightmare. This time the dream was not quite as eerie, but it did take off in the same manner but without the same intensity. The intensity was not as severe, but the message was still the same, get moving in your purpose. I remember a person saying that God gives us a purpose to walk out and if we do not walk it out; He will give it to someone else who will. That message had struck a chord in me. I wondered about these two eerie dreams. The one thing that each dream had in common was that I knew God was prompting me to get moving in my purpose. Yet, I could not seem to get it accomplished.

There was no fire or urgency to get moving in my purpose until the second nightmarish dream.

I understood my purpose was to write this book. Writing this book seemed like a long-drawn-out tiresome effort that had left me more frustrated than fruitful. I wanted to write the book, but I did not put much effort into making it happen. I enjoyed telling the story, and I told the story to everyone who would listen. God had done some awesome things in my life, yet I had not written them down. His awesomeness needed to be shared. I believe that I was to share the way He moved in my life during this *Season*. However, transcribing these thoughts to paper had become one unsuccessful attempt after the other.

Let me just say that I will never laugh at the Israelites stiff-neck jokes again. I could not believe I was doing exactly what they were doing, not being obedient to the direction that God had purposed for me. I had more reasons why I could not get this book written. I thought of the million things that I needed to do daily and the list just never stopped. After all, I got to eat, right? I got to take a shower, right? I have to do volunteer work, right? I got to do my hair, right? I got to feed and walk my dog, right? I got to clean up after myself, right? I have to do laundry, right? I have to keep my house in order, right? I have to cook, right? I have to go to my place of employment, right? I have to put gas in my car, right? I have to buy groceries, right? I have to drive people to places who cannot get there on their own, right? I have to read the mail, and pay my bills, right? I have to deal with traffic, drive to the train station, and catch the Metro to work, right? Everyone knows that these things are time-consuming, right? I have to, I have to, I have to, and the list goes on and on and on. There was never a perfect time to stop and write because there was always something I had to do. As I ponder the list above, I realized that all of these were unjustifiable excuses. I made time for the things I wanted to do—not necessarily what I needed to do. I remembered a pastor saying:

> "Tell me how your time is spent, and I will tell you your true desires."

Writing this book was not my true desire, it was not even a true want. It was something I know I should do, but I was not willing to jump in because I had no real desire to move in that direction. Yet, I knew in my heart that I was supposed to write this book. The question that kept resounding in my head was: "why have I not written the book?" To write or not to write was the question and for far too long not to write was winning.

It has taken me years but with the nudging from God and His patience, I am finally writing this book. There has been an extremely long lagging gap from the start to the finish of this book. Once I thought I was finished, I had some people review my book—there comments gave me pause. I was grateful for their invaluable input that led to reviewing, revising, rethinking, rewriting, and reconstructing the book again.

I was back tapping the keyboard and pressing my way to get it done. I purposely shut the door on Mr. Excuse, Cousin Distraction, and Uncle Interruption. All I can say is laptop don't fail me now! This calls for a double-forecast!

FORECAST

Today the pollen count is extremely high and threatening an unhealthy atmospheric index. Stay indoors and breathe life into the book you are writing. It is time to walk out of the nightmare and walk into the divine purpose of the night-aware (messages)!

Don't judge a nightmarish dream by its ugly content, there may be a message there. Instead, heed the words from Laini Taylor's quote:

"Turn your nightmares into fireflies and catch them in a jar." —Bulkrate.com

That way when it is time to release them and let them go, you will have the power to do just that!

Severe thunderstorms will produce damaging winds gushing from 50 to 60 mph. A clear warning to get moving quickly into your purpose or—well we don't want to know about the or!

Tap, tap, tap, go my fingers across the keyboard of my laptop.
I believe someone may be waiting for this book!

SUMMER SOLSTICE
Sunny, Sweltering, and Shade

*Now learn this lesson from the fig tree: As soon as its twigs get tender
and its leaves come out, you know that Summer is near.*
Mark 13:28 (NIV)

The *Summer* brings forth an explosion of excitement and fun. The *Summer* dances with hopes and dreams, tangos with explorations of love, salsas with endearments, and mambos with opportunities. *Summer* also brings sweat, humidity, and dewdrop drizzles from *Summer* rains.

In the *Summer,* you can glean from the **Son** who provides us light from the worldly sun. The light in the *Summer* splashes upon the results of our hard work, determination, and spiritual growth. *Summer* sends escapades of long, beautiful sun rays that strokes the skin and provides warm touches from God upon our sun-kissed face.

Just like the flowers lean in towards the sun, in this season you will bloom as you learn, listen, and lean in towards the **Son of God**. In the *Summer* season, your relationship with God is destined to grow stronger. You are walking with God, talking with God, crying out to God, being frustrated with God, and feeling comfortable sharing these frustrations with God. Most importantly, you simply enjoy being with God as much as He enjoys being with you. God is love and the joy of the Lord is our strength. There is nothing like having a relationship with God. Having a relationship with the **Son of God** will propel sunny days that will hold you up during sweltering moments as He covers and protect you with His shade.

=================== **FORECAST** ===================

Today is a bright beautiful sun-splash day with rays of hope beaming brightly as grace and mercy spread out on the wing-tips of His love.

———— ✇ ————

Catch your flight with God as the wings of His love take off.

7

Unbound Season

THE PRUNING

How do you explain unbound to anyone who thinks they are free— but truly are not? Most people are not aware that they are bound. Becoming unbound is a process that begins with the mindset. The process for me had not been easy but had been worth the invaluable lessons that I learned along the way. Every encounter along this journey had brought an aspect of truth into my life. The truth can be hard to recognize, especially if you had been bamboozled into believing lies. With lies running rampant at the speed of lightning, it was difficult to immediately discern the truth. I wondered—what exactly was the truth? This question had me bound.

Indeed, I was bound in so many areas of my life. I was bound with half-truths. I was bound with assumptions. I was bound by opinions and judgments. I was bound by hatred and prejudice. I was bound with unforgiveness. I was bound with complaints and excuses. I was bound with little fibs and big lies as if there is a difference. I was bound with lack and low self-esteem. I was bound with past, present, and future hurts. I was bound with questions that were begging to be released. I was bound with the fear of approaching an Almighty God, knowing that I was unworthy. I was blindly walking around bound with invisible chains of fear, shame, guilt, self-hate, and many other forms of entrapments that continuously had me bound.

To boot, my prayer life was bound. I did not get the concept of prayer. I had prayed in the past as I cried out in heartfelt urgency, as that just came naturally to me. However, to stop and think about prayer, especially in front of someone was very difficult. I watched a lot of people pray and they prayed elegantly. I tried to mimic them, but I could not make that happen. I wanted so badly to be able to pray like them. I tried to pray but it was always a struggle. If I prayed out loud, I would stumble over my words and I would sound like a bumbling nitwit. My prayers were one-liners or a couple of sentences. My prayer-life felt inadequate. No matter how hard I tried to pray, my mind would wander and I would quickly lose focus. I wondered if my prayer-life was inadequate because of all of my past mistakes, not to mention my outright disobedience. I did things that I knew were wrong. I carried a cup of guilt around as a reminder of my sins. I struggled with whether or not God could forgive me when I knew I had done things blatantly wrong by intentionally ignoring what I knew to be right. Needless to say, my prayer-life was bound.

In one of my conversations with God, I asked Him to place godly friends in my life. God in His loving-kindness answered this prayer request by doing just that. Each person that he placed in my life was instrumental in my walk with Christ. One such person was a beautiful *Woman of God* named Nora Jones. Her spiritual guidance began the unveiling of my brokenness. She could see plainly what I could not. Many time things are often hidden in us, whereas other people can see clearly what we cannot. I was introduced to Nora on a morning prayer-call which I was invited by Melissa (Jerdon). There were four of us: Melissa, Nora, Mary Jones, and myself. We met weekly every morning Monday through Friday. I did not know what to expect because I had never taken part in a prayer-call. The initial call put me at ease because everyone was so welcoming, and they were okay with me just listening as opposed to me praying. I always felt inadequate praying, and no one needed to know that, and I was not about to share that information.

Through the prayer-call, our friendship blossomed, and we would talk with each other often, even one-on-one at various times throughout the day. Each one of them spoke life into my current situation, which at the time was breast cancer—this situation had me bound.

One day, the *Woman of God* took me to the school of hard knocks. Nora called me because she was deeply concerned about my comments after the morning prayer-call. I began my spiel about my life as I saw it. I was complaining, and complaining, and complaining! I was bound with woe-its-me complaints. It was one of my greatest self-destructive acts at the time. She quietly listened to my sing-song complaints and allowed me to get it all out. When I finished, she simply said:

"Would you like for me to answer you truthfully concerning the situation?"

I have to admit the question had me perplexed because what I was speaking was the truth. I wondered to myself, what part was she not hearing? After all, I am the one who has been wronged. The way she asked the question, made me leery and inquisitive at the same time. Thus, I opted to say, "I want to hear what you have to say." Truthfully, part of me did not want to hear what she had to say because of how she posed the question. Nora's question and her response below had me bound.

"You may not like what I am about to say to you, but it is out of love and it is for your good. The first thing I need you to do is to take your mouth off that situation and begin to pray for that individual. I know you have been hurt and what you feel is real but that is not going to help you. Whenever you think of that individual say a prayer as simple as LORD bless the person. You cannot speak negativity and positivity at the same time. The second thing I want you to do is to pray these words "Lord, show me, me!"

All I could do was listen as tears streamed down my face. The tears poured out like an overflowing dam as I accepted the godly advice from this beautiful *Woman of God*. I thanked God that He sent Nora on my path. This beautiful *Woman of God* loved me enough to tell me the truth. It hurt but her delivery was out of pure love and it was exactly what I needed. Now, I needed to follow through with her godly advice and that thought had me bound.

The advice from the *Woman of God* never left me. Whenever the individual popped up in my head, I would send up a prayer of blessings. This would be my first lesson in praying for my enemies and frenemies. Believe me when I say that this was not an easy process and it did not happen overnight. The prayers were very short and simple. I uttered the prayer, "Lord bless the person," just as the *Woman of God* had directed me. I did this every time I wanted to complain about the individual. Needless to say, I was sending up prayers of blessings for that individual all day long. One day I encountered the individual and the venom and hate were gone. I just looked up, smiled, and thanked God. God was melting away at the icy hatred in my heart for the individual that once had me bound.

I followed through with the second part of the advice which was to pray the prayer "Lord, show me, me!" One day, I was on my knees praying to God and He answered my prayer of "Lord, show me, me!" The answer had me mortified, and I could not stop crying. He showed me who I really was, and it was not pretty. I apologized profusely and prayed to God to get rid of those horrific traits. What He showed me about myself had me bound.

As God was pulling back the layers to reveal who I was, this began the process of purging and pruning me to become a better me. I thank God for this group and for these beautiful women. I have since lost contact with most of these women, however; I will never forget the lessons I have learned, the way they welcomed me, and how God used that particular prayer group in that particular season to grow my spiritual muscles. God was pruning my tough heart that was likened to the Georgia red clay—rough, hard, and stubborn. These ladies were pivotal in helping me to understand what it would take for me to become—unbound!

On my journey to becoming unbound, I desired to develop a personal relationship with God. However, I was not quite sure how to navigate my way to Him. I tried to read the King James Version (KJV) **Bible** which was hard to understand. I was elated to find the New International Version (NIV) which was an easier translation. I desired to draw nearer to God. I knew that God could see right into the heart and matter of my soul. I could easily talk with God, but I wanted our conversations to be a two-way dialogue. I wanted to be able to listen and hear from Him as well. I wanted my lifestyle to incorporate sincere heartfelt authentic prayers, and I was not sure how to go about it. I came across a quote by Charles H. Spurgeon that spoke to me:

> "If your day is hemmed with prayer, it is less likely to unravel."

I desired that my days be hemmed with prayer. This quote made me think about the hem of Jesus's garment that the lady with the issue of blood had reached out to touch. I needed to get to the spiritual hem of His garment so that I could **draw close to Him**.

I designed a prayer board. Each month I added a new prayer target for the current month while still praying for all the previous month's targets. The more I sought God, the stronger my desire to draw near to him in prayer. I took these words by Corrie Ten Boom to heart when I saw them:

> "What wings are to a bird, and sails to a ship so is prayer to the soul."

There was an urging desire within me that longed for God. I was eager to build a prayer-life and **establish an authentic relationship with Him**.

In seeking a relationship, I would find time to sit in His presence. I affirm the author's comment that stated:

> "There is only one thing that is needed and that one thing is being in the presence of God."

Mary got it right when Jesus came to their home. Martha was busying about, which is a normal part of hospitality. Yet, there is only one thing truly needed. The one thing needed is to **sit at the feet of Jesus and to glean from Him.**

I wanted to know His voice. I wanted to hear His voice. I wanted to listen to His voice and be wrapped in the beauty of His loving voice. I began to talk with God daily about nothing in particular. I was simply enjoying these small conversations here and there. I especially enjoyed the times when He would put a smile on my face. I was enjoying my talks with God and **spending sweet precious time with Him.**

One day, I was sitting with my **Bible** open, trying to listen to God through His Word. Let me tell you, there is nothing like being taught by God Himself. There was an explosion of revelation and truth that brought streams of water trickling down my face. I began to write down what I was hearing. I could not believe how much revelation came in that period (about four hours). My desire to get to know God mirrored Jeremiah 20:9 (NIV) when he stated: *His Word is in my heart like a fire, a fire shut up in my bones*—**I truly loved the day when I was taught by Him.**

I generally walk my dog three times a day. I wanted to use these walks to solely focus wholeheartedly on God. No cellphone, music, etc. I just wanted to walk and talk with Him, like He was my dear closest friend. I understood that I could bring my petitions to Him, but I wanted this time to be different. I purposefully set my mind to solely focus on God. Yet, I could not get to the end of the block without mental distractions. I would lose my focus and my mind would wander on anything but God. I marveled at the busyness of my mind. So, I tried it again and again, but before I could get to the end of the block, my mind was elsewhere. I was feeling a little discouraged because **I just wanted to talk with Him**.

I kept wondering what could I do to keep my mind focused on God. I began thanking Him for things and surprisingly I was able to make it to the end of the block. I was so excited that I repeated the process over and over again. And this pattern would follow until I returned home. This is how I started learning to keep my focus on God. My walks initially started with the *Lord's Prayer* and generally ended with me thanking Him for any and everything. I can truly say that I was **enjoying my walks with Him**.

Our walks became special to me. I wanted to expand our conversations and build upon our friendship. I remember a game I played with my children when they were young. We called it, the *Alphabet Game.* We played this game a lot, especially on long road trips. I thought, maybe I could play the *Alphabet Game* with my Abba Father. As I was strolling along and thinking about the *Alphabet Game*, I decided to think of all the ways that I could worship, praise, and thank God from A-Z. The game kept our conversation flowing for days because I would not skip over a letter. I was seeking words that describe the essence of God. I enjoyed the *Alphabet Game* which **kept me engaged with Him**.

As trivial as this game may sound, it became a fun and pleasant time with God. One day I was walking and talking to Him concerning the *Alphabet Game* and He made me laugh out loud. I quickly looked around because I did not have my headphones on. I looked up to God and said silently, "You can't do that, people are going to think I am a nut-case." Oh, how I loved that day when God made me laugh and put a smile on my face☺. I continued to sniggle trying hard to keep it in because it was too funny. Laughing with God does not happen as often as I would like it to, but when it does it blesses me tremendously. Who knew God had a sense of humor? I did not, but it was soooooo nice to find out that He does. I looked up Scriptures on laughter and found the following:

Genesis 21:6 (KJV)
*And Sarah said, God hath made me to **laugh**,
so that all that hear will laugh with me.*

Job 8:21 (NIV)
*He will yet fill your mouth with **laughter***
and your lips with shouts of joy.
Psalms 2:4 (NIV)
*The One enthroned in heaven **laughs**;*

I had no idea that God could be fun. To say that I had a lot to learn would be an understatement. This was one of my best discoveries about God because I love to laugh, and I especially **loved to laugh with Him**.

On our walks together, the *Alphabet Game* became **our thing** for a *Season*. As unpretentious as this game was, it was so much fun, and it led to much dialogue in our conversations. I would ask God questions such as: "What do you think? Or how about this? Or do these words truly describe Your attributes?" I was enjoying my walks and discussions with Him. One such discussion led me to have a favorite letter of the alphabet, which was the letter "**I**," based on 2 Corinthians 9:15 (NIV): *Thanks be to God for His indescribable gift.* God gave Jesus to us as an indescribable gift. How can anyone explain the beauty of that inexpressible, irrefutable, inexplicable gift? When I think about this gift, it touches me deeply because I know it was done out of pure agape love. I can honestly say that I was truly **falling in love with Him**.

Alphabet Game

A | Awesome
    B | Beautiful
        C | Compassionate
            D | Dear (deeply affectionate and cherished by me)
E | Eternal
    F | Faithful
        G | Gracious
            H | Holy
I | Indescribable (my favorite word to describe God who cannot be described)
    J | Just
        K | Kind

L | Loving

M | Magnificent

N | Nurturing

O | Omnipotent

P | Powerful

Q | Quintessential

R | Righteous

S | Savior

T | Trustworthy

U | Unique

V | Valiant

W | Wise

X | Xnihilo (created out of nothing)

Y | Yahweh

Z | Zealous

The *Alphabet Game* led to the birth of several new songs. One song was: "Lord I Want to be in Your Presence." The walks started because I wanted to be in His presence. I wanted to get to know Him for myself. As I had mentioned before, God had given me two songs during my plight, but as the years progressed, He would bless me with over eighty songs. Some with lyrical tunes and others written without any musical tones. More than anything I wanted to write *God's Love* upon my heart, whether through music or literature. I wanted to be the pen that He used to transcribe His thoughts to the world. Being in His presence touched my heart immensely! The *Alphabet Game* moved me to **deeply explore with Him**.

One of the explorations from spending time with God led me to seek the names of God. The more I learned about God's names, the more I discovered who God is as the Creator of Heaven and Earth. I researched the names of God from A–Z; however, I could not find every letter of the English alphabet. The bolded lines are the letters that I could not find, hence I replaced it with an English word that spoke to His character. My research shows that the names of God are spelled differently but have the same meaning depending on the origin of the word such as Kanna and Quanna; Yireh and Jireh; Roi and Rai; or Sali and Sel'i. The tasking was not an easy find, but definitely worth the time and effort to learn the names of God. Psalms 9:10 (NIV) states: *Those who know Your name trust in You, for You, LORD, have never forsaken those who seek You.* **My truest desire was to sincerely seek Him.**

Names of God Alphabetically

A | Adonai: The Lord, My Great Lord

B | Bashamayim: The Lord God in Heaven (*Elohim Bashamayim*)

C | Chasdi: God of my Kindness, Goodness, and Faithfulness (*Elohei Chasdi*)

D | De'ot: The God of Knowledge (*El De'ot*)

E | Elohim: The All-Powerful One, Creator *(the plural name of El)*

F | **Father:** *Creator of Heaven and Earth, Supreme*

G | Gemuwal: The Lord God of Recompense (*Jehovah El Gemuwal*)

H | Hakabodh: The God of Glory (*El Hakabodh*)

I | Immeku: The Lord is with You (*Jehovah Immeku*)

J | Jireh: The Lord Will Provide (*Jehovah Jireh*)

K | Kedoshim: Holy God (*Elohim Kedoshim*)

L | **LORD:** *Master, Authority, Sovereign*

M | Ma'uzzi: God of my Strength (*Elohei Ma'uzzi*)

N | Nissi: The Lord is my Banner (*Jehovah Nissi*)

O | Olam: Our Everlasting God (*Elohenu Olam*)

P | Paraclete: Holy Spirit, Counselor

Q | Qanna: The Jealous God (*El Qanna*)

R | Roi: The God Who Sees (*El Roi*)

S | Sali: God my Rock (*El Sali*)

T | Tsaba: The Lord God of Hosts (*Jehovah Elohim Tsaba*)

U | Uzam: The Lord's Strength in Trouble (*Jehovah 'Uzam*)

V | **Victor:** *Conqueror, Champion, The Greatest*

W | **Wisdom:** *Sagacity, Perceptive, Insightful, Discerning*

X | Xnihilo: Out of Nothing

Y | Yeshua: The Lord God of my *Salvation* (*Jehovah Elohim Yeshua*)

Z | **Zealous:** *Fervent, Passionate, Devoted, Keen*

Okay, so you get the point. My real reason for sharing this is to let you know that God will meet you where you are—no matter how insignificant or trivial the conversation may seem. Because God is love, He will lovingly engage in a conversation with you, simply because He sees what is in your heart. I struggled for years to conversate—on-going—with God. I would say good morning, good night, and how are you, to name a few. I cannot say I waited for a response. I would say it and keep it moving. Now, I can honestly say I can have an actual conversation with God. Most walks start with praising Him alphabetically for who He is. From this point, the conversation can go anywhere from prayer to supplication, to confession, to thanksgiving. Ahhhhh, it's such an amazing feeling just *to be close to Him.*

Another one of my creative promptings was inspired when I came across Psalms 33:9 (HCSB) which says: *For He spoke, and it came into being; He commanded, and it came into existence.* The scriptural numbers caught my attention because I was born at 3:39 am on a Monday. As I looked at Psalms 33:9, I decided to do a 3-3-9 journey of the entire **Bible**. The journey took 39 days. In each book, I highlighted the 3rd Chapter and the 3rd and 9th verses. Where there were less than three books, I had to become even more creative such as highlighting the 339th word, and where that was not possible, it was a countdown to sentences, punctuations, etc. I journaled the 3-3-9 Scriptures to see how I could apply them to my life, extract a lesson, receive confirmation, conviction, or encouragement. I enjoyed this project. It was another creative way to read the **Bible** and just *hang out with Him.*

I like being creative and amid many innovative ideas, my creativity brought me closer to God. There are so many ways to connect with God. I tried to fill my day with God as much as I could. I wanted my day to be wrapped around God as opposed to having Him as the second, third or last fiddle in my life. On this journey, I refused to allow anyone to prohibit me from seeking God, especially since I realized that He is my most invaluable treasure. The list below is some creative ways that I used in conjunction with seeking God. You can use my list below or create your own. Just make spending time with God, a daily priority!

1. Create an annual scriptural theme and set personal and spiritual goals for the year around the theme.
2. Design a prayer board with a declaration stating that you will recite daily such as *I am* statements.
3. Write love letters to God, He wrote you one when He gave you the **Bible**.
4. Biblical coloring book (relaxing)
5. Listening to sermons and asking God to show you what you need to take away from the lectures.
6. Talk with God as you read the *Word of God*.
7. Create a "Thankful" journal—choose gratitude and record it.
8. Watch TV with God and/or go to the movies with God.
9. Take walks with God.

One of the hardest things I had to learn to do was to listen to the correction and conviction from my Heavenly Father. He would use many resources to show me areas that needed to be corrected. It would hurt, and although receiving the truth can hurt, it will always be for your good. He had moved me to pray for my enemies (foes) and forgive my frenemies (betrayers). I would have never done these things unless God had gotten ahold of me. This was not an easy task, but it was a much-needed action for me to grow my spiritual muscles. It was a **blessing to grow up in Him.**

I would never forget this girl who I grew up with had greeted me very kindly and I snubbed her with a nasty attitude because of the venomous hatred I had for her since we were thirteen years old. At the time, I was in my thirties—do the math—so sad! She simply said to me:

"Are you still mad at me over the incident that happened
when were thirteen years old?
Are you ever going to forgive me?"

I considered what she said. My emotions when it came to her were on autopilot. I just automatically hated her, and I made sure she automatically knew it whenever I saw her. I said to her with an adjusted attitude, "You are right, that was then, this is now, let bygones be bygones." I could not believe I had harbored such deep-rooted hatred for someone for that many years. I wanted this part of me to be removed. When you desire to do the right thing, God will always show you your progress. Years later, when I saw her again, I was able to greet her with no venom. Praise God! My greatest growth came when I surrendered to the will of God. His conviction is love and His love is truth! The book of John says it like this: *But when the Spirit of truth comes, He will guide you into all truth*—John 16:13 (MEV). It may not be easy doing the right thing, but it is worth it because doing the right thing develops you into having the right character. And a right character is a character that can be used by God. I reveled in my **obedience towards Him.**

Succinctly, I continue seeking various Scriptures and ask God to show me how I could continue to improve and grow through *His Word.* I was peering through the eyes of God and listening to His heartbeat of correction, confirmation, conviction, and reassurance, reflection, restoration. Learning to heed God's direction is vital to the type of relationship you will establish with God. I leaned in to hear Him with my heart as **He opened my ears to listen to Him.**

To be bound or not to be bound is the question. And the answer is only God can truly unbind the bound! In Psalms 44:3, the Scripture talks about victory from God and not by the hands of man: *It was not by their sword that they won the land, nor did their arm bring them victory; it was Your right hand, Your arm, and the light of Your face, for You loved them.*" Our victory in becoming unbound is won when we come and sit daily in the presence of God which inevitably **brought me into a relationship with Him.**

PRAYER

Lord touch my heart and let me always remember Your precious Word that says: *But the Word of God is not bound*—2 Timothy 2:9 (ESV).

FORECAST

There will be early morning rainfalls with noontime thunderstorms. The rest of the day will be partly cloudy with the sun peeking through with streaming rays of light.

Prayer break chains—clank, clank, clank. I hear several chains breaking as they hit the ground and it is the precious sound of freedom, the sound of becoming unbound! Walk speedily into your purpose that awaits you on destiny lane.

Unfulfilled Season

THE PROBLEM

Smell? Odor? Scent? Not necessarily a bad scent, but an odorific reeking that lingers in a particular space. That is how I associated the atmosphere of a hospital. There is always an unpleasant scent that is quite irritable. I understand that the nature of a hospital cannot have fresh blossoms coming out of the vents but does the scent have to be—hmmmmm—whatever it is? It is not quite a stench, although it can be, generally, it is just a specific odor tied to hospitals and you know you are in one when it welcomes you at the door. In this specific case, the entrance door to the chemotherapy suite.

The chemo suite is where the transfusion of medication is administered to each individual. I feared chemotherapy for all the stories foretold by so many people. I thought it odd that they would refer to a section of the hospital as a suite; as if you are going somewhere relaxing, which of course is quite the contrary. In the chemo suite there were many lounge chairs and beside each lounger was a stand where the intravenous bags stood ready to be inserted into its next victim of prey. Most people had ports placed in them, but some braved their veins and that was a hideous sight.

Albeit the atmosphere, the technicians, nurses, and staff all were very accommodating and took great care of everyone in the suite. The treatments varied from person to person. The length of the treatment depended on the type of cancer and the stage of cancer. My treatments were about four hours every three weeks. At times, the suite was an eerie quiet. Some would be asleep. I tried to go to sleep but was unsuccessful. Some came with caring people whether with family or a friend. Some were alone and that saddened my heart. I was grateful that I had my mother with me, and I thank God that she never left my side during the entire process.

The chemo treatments are extremely harsh on the body. The battle is real. And as I mentioned before the red liquid fire (chemo) is no joke. The red liquid fire had no mercy on its prey. It makes you sick to your stomach to the point where you are constantly vomiting up the results of this red liquid fire. You are forced to carry a barf bag because the vomiting has no set schedule. It simply comes when it is ready. It makes no apologies and could care less who you are, whom you are with, or where you are at any specified time. To boot, your taste buds are weakened, and you carry a disgusting taste in your mouth that just lingers no matter how much you gargle or brush your teeth. After each treatment, I had to take additional medication to fight off possible infections because the red liquid fire damages so many of your good cells that are needed during this fierce battle.

Cancer is no respecter of persons. In the chemo suite, there was a lot of somberness as well as hopefulness. Everyone was at the battleline for whatever type of cancer they had. We were all trying to hold on to any bit of hope that we could. Ironically, the darkest place held the hope of most of the patients inside of the IV (intravenous) bag; yet I knew that my hope needed to be anchored in God. I knew that God was not limited to how He heals anyone. I had to trust God that this journey I was embarking upon was in His mighty Omnipotent hands.

As I mentioned before, my mom was with me every step of the way. To state that my mom was like a *Supermom* without the Clark Kent cape would be an understatement. My father and I both had cancer at the same time and I felt bad about sharing my plight but I knew I needed my mom in this *Season*. I thank God that my mom was able to be there for me. She drove me to every treatment. She lived thirty minutes away. She would leave her house and drive thirty minutes to come and pick me up, only to have to drive back the same way she came about twenty-five minutes to get onto the Beltway. Once on the Beltway, it was another fifty minutes commute to my destination. The entire trip from her house to the chemo treatment center was about two hours to just get me there and she did this roundtrip. She never complained or asked for gas monies. She simply told me these words that I will never ever forget:

"And this too shall pass!"

My mom ran two households during my illness and I have no idea how she did it. My kids were participating in sports and activities and because of her, they never missed anything. She had to keep up with me, my father (who also had cancer), and my kids. Looking back, I do not think I ever truly thanked her or told her how much I appreciated her for being there for me and the kids. This was one of the darkest *Seasons* of my life. God had blessed me with the most beautiful mother in the world. So, let me stop to just say it now: "Thank you mom for being by my side when I needed you the most. I truly love you. God gave you to me as a gift, and I thank my Heavenly Father for you being that beautiful gift, wrapped in a beautiful package of love, called Mom!"

One day I was in Patapsco Flea Market near Baltimore and saw a picture with the same words that my mom spoke to me. I immediately felt the need to purchase that picture. In the picture was an angel sitting down and hugging her knees drawn up to her chest. I pictured the angel praying and holding on to hope. The words inscribed on the picture spoke to my heart because those words were the exact words that my mom spoke to me:

"And this too shall pass!"

The angel in the picture represents my mother. She was carrying a heavy load but never revealed it. She was the guardian angel I needed in this *Season*. God kept her and she kept me. I thanked God for the mother He gave me.

My days seemed dreary. I was in a state of trying to believe what I could not see. This was very hard since nothing around me spelled possible. The signs of death were lurking from every corner of my mind. Sometimes I would feel so broken down and sad that if I stayed there too long it would have turned into a deep depression. God had sent an abundance of resources my way: from Scriptures to music, to literature, to sermons, to DVDs, and people. I did not realize it at the time, but the resources were divinely orchestrated for the battle in which I was currently engaged (cancer). Some days the storms were unbearable, and others were tolerable. There was a tug-of-war struggle going on inside of me: belief-fear, belief-fear, belief-fear. I knew that I needed to remain in a posture to **War Up** at any moment. Now, where did that come from—**War Up?** Hmmm, what does that even mean?

War up! I heard the words **War Up** in my spirit. I went to the internet to see how it was defined. I could not find anything. I asked God what is **War Up**? And why did these words come to me? Did I hear correctly? I believe I heard it correctly because that is exactly what I wrote down. Yet, the internet yielded nothing on this catchphrase. I contemplated these words over and over again in my head. I had discerned that **War Up** is a state of preparedness for whatever situation or *Season* an individual is currently in or may be coming into. Simply put, to **War Up** is to stand on the *Word of God* fully and believe—no matter what may come. It is a state of mind that God uses to equip us for the battle. God was preparing me to learn the art of how to **War Up!** God etched the following strategy upon my heart:

- **Face it** | Opposition
- **Feel it** | Emotions
- **Free it** | Release
- **Find it** | Truth

Face the Opposition

I had to learn to deal with the mountains that were standing in front of me. I had to face my opposition head-on whether I wanted to or not. This is an order—not an option!

War Up and *Forward March!*

Feel the Emotions

I had to learn to acknowledge my feelings. It is okay to feel fear and to recognize how that fear makes your emotions react; but you cannot stay there. I had to learn to redirect my focus!

War Up and *About Face!*

Free the Release

I had to learn the art of releasing negative emotions back to the pit where they came from. Do not allow negativity to stand in your presence. Shoo negativity away!

War Up and *Dismiss!*

Find the Truth

I had to learn to continuously seek the face of God. As you seek Him, He will reveal many truths to you. He is the Commander and Chief. Our eyes should always be on Him. Find your rest in His truth while dwelling in His presence.

War Up and *At Ease!*

God used many resources that assisted me to **War Up**. The most precious resources I found were in a treasure chest called the **Bible**. Inside the **Bible** are priceless hidden gems for anyone who is sincerely seeking God. The gems are likened to a priceless rare blue pearl found on the Island of Tahiti. The treasure box is hidden out in the open for everyone. Many people have the treasure box, yet they won't open it. The treasure box teaches us that: *My people are destroyed for lack of* knowledge" (Hosea 4:6 ESV). And the ISV declares: *My people are destroyed because they lack knowledge of me.* I love this version because the truth is you can amass all the knowledge in the world but if you do not have a relationship with God, you have missed the mark. He is the One who is the author of all things, knowledge included. When you begin to seek God with your whole heart, His treasures are revealed. They were always there, but you have to seek Him for your eyes to be opened to see them. As you seek God, you will build a strong personable relationship with Him. And He will reveal things that you do not know through His treasure box, the **Bible**. Seeking God first (Matthew 6:33), can never be an option, it is truly a promised privilege. When you seek God first, the dynamics of the relationship between you and God will enlighten you to grow to another level.

God's treasures of gems are gifted for His children to find. Each gem reflects what is in you. The gems teach you about the truth of God and yourself. There are gems hidden in coal such as diamonds, or gems hidden in rocks such as agate. To get to the gem, you will have to allow God to chip away at the outer core to discover the inner core of your soul. Your outer core is what you think you are, and your inner core is who you are. As you move into this discovery, you will grow deeper into a relationship with God. God's flawless hands are the cloth that purifies each gem. God will take the unbuffered gems and buff them, polish them, and restore them to their original luster. Once the gem has been restored to its original luster, God will set it inside a prong (mind) so that its light is no longer refracted (bent/broken); but it will be reflected (bounced back to a healing) for all to see the glory of God manifested. Some things may be difficult but remember it is only for a time and *Season*. The trials are merely a part of the pruning process to develop you and make you stronger. God uses everyday things to teach us the *Secrets of His Love.* The gems are our inheritance from our Abba Father. Anyone can hold a gemstone in their hand. It is not what you are holding but what you are doing with what God has placed in your hand. God wants us to: *Establish the work of our hands*—Psalms 90:17 (ESV). I once heard a pastor say:

"God is the hidden treasure that you have been looking for and you didn't even know it."

There are many gems (Scriptures) in the **Bible**. I desired to learn about these precious gems in the **Bible** and wanted to sincerely get to know God. I prayed, "Lord, help me to War Up with Your Word." God in His loving-kindness took the time to show me my gems from His treasure chest, the **Bible**; which was instrumental in my character growth and my spiritual development. Finding the gems are precious; however, allowing God to buff and polish you where it is rough can be quite tasking. Only God knows what each of us needs and when we need it. God gave me twelve gems that were instrumental in developing a relationship with Him. God buffed and polished each gem as I drew near to Him. Some people may have some of these same gems or God may give other individuals a different gem. We each grow differently in our relationship with God. Only God can provide what each of us needs! These are the *gems* that I needed. Ask God what *gems you are in need of so that He can* buffed and polished your character traits.

War Up * Treasure Chest
The Truth of God's Word

Bible Jewel Treasure Chest

1. **Amethyst of Acceptance** | Accept Christ (Romans 10:8–10)
   - Many people reading this book have already accepted Christ into their lives. You may advance to number two. This is my journey so the story for you may be quite different. Once I accepted Christ the floodgates opened up and many mysteries were revealed. Such as writing songs with musical compositions, authorship, and a blooming relationship with God. I also began to see life from a different purview, none of these were a smidgen of thought before becoming **saved**.
2. **Beryl of Bible** | Read the **Bible** (Joshua 1:8)
   - Many Pastors only want you to read King James Version (KJV). I struggled with the KJV. I am not saying to discount it, but for me with a minuscule understanding of God; I could not grasp that version and it became very frustrating to me. I was introduced to the New International Version (NIV) which was translated into today's vernacular. I have since read many versions along with the KJV and my knowledge of *His Word* has expanded.
3. **Sapphire of Study** | Know the Word for yourself (2 Timothy 2:15)
   - Reading God's Word is wonderful. I was amazed at how many Christians do not read the **Bible**. Many regurgitate what the Pastor says which can be good, but how can you study yourself approve if you do not verify that what you hear is the actual *Word of God*. Don't be bamboozled. I have been there, done that, and wore the hat. The only way to truly know God is to read and study God's Word.
4. **Quartz of Quiet Time** | Spend time with God (Psalm 46:10)
   - This was very hard for me to do initially but worth the pressing in the long run. Today I cannot imagine not talking to God daily. This is no longer an option for me. My favorite time with God is when I laugh. I love to laugh, and I love to laugh with God. Spending time with God is a privilege and a pleasure. Being still in His presence is an honor.

5. **Peridot of Purging** | Rend your heart to God (Joel 2:13)
    - Cleansing and conviction were hard but once I had learned to surrender; it took me to new heights with God. When I did not feel like I could submit, I asked for help from the Holy Spirit. I remembered wanting to get someone back who had hurt me. The individual made me so mad. I was talking to God about the hurtful situation and I said to God—I know you would want me to do X, Y, Z because of what the individual had done to me. Then I said, "Lord unless You tell me otherwise, then I am going to do X, Y, Z." I sat down with the **Bible** and I opened up to Obadiah 15 which summed up went like this: *extend the same mercy that You would want a person to extend to you. I did not want* to talk to God anymore that day. It just didn't seem right. This Scripture was so hard for me to accept because it seemed so unfair. Yet, I accepted His direction. Obedience was not easy and had caused a major dam flow of tears, yet; it was the absolute best thing for me. When God tells you to do something it is because He loves you and it is always for your good even when it does not seem like it, all will be good in the end. He is your vindicator.
6. **Ruby of Remembrance** | Memorize Scripture in your heart (Psalms 119:11)
    - It is crucial to be battle-ready at all times (**War up**). When I was going into surgery, it was Scriptures from memory that got me through. Attacks do not give you advance notice. Having the Scriptures stored in your memory bank is a powerful safeguard to ward off unexpected attacks.
7. **Pearls of Prayer** | Pray continuously (1 Thessalonian 5:17)
    - When I read Luke 11:1 (NIV), it spoke directly to my heart: *Lord teach us to pray.* This has been a sincere desire as well as a personal struggle. God began to show me that there was no one way to pray. I would pray Scriptures because I did not want my flesh involved. Sometimes, I would journal my prayers. I would kneel and pray. Other times I would draw my prayers. I would go on prayer walks, attend

prayer parties, participate in prayer watch, and attend prayer conferences. Each of these prayer venues only brought me closer to God.

8. **Lapis Lazuli of Listening** | Be attentive (James 1:19)
   - I was a talker and a terrible listener. This was another area that God had to help me to develop and truth be told it is still developing. You cannot talk and listen at the same time. I had a spirit of complaining and someone called me out and said:

     > "Every time I see you, you are always complaining about something."

   - God sure knows how to get your attention. It was as if my eyes and ears stood at attention! I had to take a look at myself. I prayed to God to remove the spirit of complaining. I have not arrived, but I am not where I used to be. The ironic thing now is that I hate to hear people who have the spirit of complaining. But I show them the same mercy as God had shown to me. I have to admit that the hardcore blow from that young lady stung badly but I would not change a thing because this was a selah moment—I was growing up in God.

9. **Sardonyx of Sowing** | Sow generously and you will reap generously (2 Corinthians 9:6)
   - Being kind to hateful and evil people was a task in the making. There have been lots of failed attempts trying to sow where there was no fertile ground. However, what this was showing me was my unkind disposition towards people I did not care for and what I needed to do to change my reaction towards them. I was learning to humbly be quiet, listen, and to pray. On the flip side, I had to learn to love myself and find joy within, and that also was not an easy tasking because of my own personal self-hate that I subliminally harbored. I had so much self-hatred and

disappointments that I was miserable and bitter. All of these ugly roots had to be pulled up. I was learning to sow in unchartered territories. I used to walk around mean-mugged (not happy) and not speak. I forced myself to speak to everyone and began a wave ministry in my neighborhood. I started waving at everyone. I couldn't believe how sowing that simple act of kindness changed my entire perspective and opened up many dialogues that I would have never encountered before me incorporating this act of kindness. God was teaching me to sow the seeds that I wanted to see manifested in my life.

10. **Jasper of Judiciousness** | Prudent and discerning (Proverbs 16:23)
   - Learning to exercise prudence and discernment is still a challenge for me today. I struggle where there are fine lines involved. I have made a lot of mistakes and I have learned from them as well. It is a well-known fact that experience is the best teacher. I beg to differ and agree with a different author that said:

      "Learning from others' experience is the better teacher."

   - And if you want an even better experience, seek God first in all things. It took quite a while for me to grasp this concept. The Holy Spirit will always be our best experience, teacher, and counselor.

11. **Chalcedony of Covering** | **War Up** daily (Ephesians 6:10–18)
   - Learning to dress up with the *Word of God* is a day-to-day experience. The Word does not change but our circumstances will change. Being prepared for varying situations that await you at every corner can be mind-boggling if you are not mentally cloaked, wrapped, and covered by the *Word of God*. Just like we have to wear our PPE (personal protective equipment) during the coronavirus pandemic; we need to put on our spiritual PPE daily. Our spiritual PPE is

found in Psalms 91 where the protective covering is God Almighty being our refuge, fortress, shield, and buckler. And it is found in Ephesians 6 where we have to armor up with the belt of *Truth*, the breastplate of *Righteousness*, feet of *Peace*, shield of *Faith*, sword of the Spirit, helmet of *Salvation*, and *Prayer*.

12. **Diamond of Doing** | Be a doer and walk it out (James 1:22).
    - Christians have a beautiful gift to share with the world, but many people do not know that we are Christians because our light does not shine from within. What drew me personally to Christianity was the light that was shining in a beautiful *Woman of God* (Adriana). Her love of God was so beautiful that I wanted to experience that same love. People should know who we are by the light we emit. My heart's desire is for God to help me to walk it out, and be a doer of the Word and not just a hearer. I desire to be God's vessel of light that others may see God in me, just as I saw God in Adriana.

This is not an exhaustive listing. God guided me to the gemstones that I needed for my development. These gems became my foundation to build my faith. The foundation had to be set firmly in its place within my heart. It is one thing to say something, but it's another thing to believe what you say. Aligning my heart with God's heart was my ultimate desire. I had to learn to appreciate each gem that spoke to my heart from God's treasure box. Once the foundational gems were etched upon my heart, God began preparing me for the next phase which was character development.

War Up * Toolbox

Character Development

God in His loving-kindness began patiently working on me, shaping me, and molding me for His purpose. He used many resources to enhance my character development. Some of them were from *His Word*, from people, from pictures, from nature, through literature, through sermons, through experience, and many other channels—there was not just one way.

Inside the toolbox was everything I needed for my character building. My toolbox had been designed for me for God's purpose. That does not mean that someone else could not glean or benefit from my toolbox. My toolbox included the following: belief, faith, forgiveness, grace, hope, joy, love, mercy, peace, praise, trust, and worship. These areas needed pruning and development. All of these areas were a struggle personally for me, yet these may not be a struggle for someone else. God will put in your toolbox exactly what you need to grow and develop areas in your life that draw you closer to Him. The beauty of the toolbox is that the tools can be built upon each other, used singularly, or as a combined effort.

- 📖 *Chisel* of **HOPE** | Jeremiah 29:11(NIV)
  - ○ *For I know the plans I have for you, declares the LORD, plans to prosper you and not to harm you, plans to give you **hope** and a future.*
    - ▪ No matter what it looks like, I had to learn that God's plan even when it hurts is the best plan for me.
    - ▪ I had to find my *hope* when I was diagnosed with breast cancer.
    - ▪ I had to learn to anchor my *hope* in Christ.
- 📖 *Box Cutter* of **BELIEF** | Mark 9:24 (NIV)
  - ○ *. . . I do **believe**; help me overcome my unbelief!*
    - ▪ You cannot waver and believe at the same time.
    - ▪ I had to learn to ask God to intercede and help me with my unbelief so that I would not waver.
    - ▪ The adversary will throw fiery darts to quell your belief; I had to remember that he is a liar.
- 📖 *Pliers* of **GRACE** | Ephesians 2:8 (NIV) (GW)
  - ○ *For it is by grace you have been saved, through faith* (NIV).
  - ○ *God saved you through faith as an act of kindness. You had nothing to do with it. Being saved is a gift from God* (GW).
    - ▪ Grace is not for sale; it is for anyone who will receive it.
    - ▪ You cannot work for grace; you can only receive grace and I had to learn to accept this priceless gift from God.
    - ▪ People will make you think God's grace is not sufficient when it truly is; I had to learn to ignore them. The cost of grace was paid at the Cross.
- 📖 *Hammer* of **FORGIVENESS** | Matthew 6:14 (NIV)
  - ○ *For if you **forgive** other people when they sin against you, your heavenly Father will also forgive you.*
    - ▪ I had to learn what forgiveness was and what it was not.
    - ▪ I was able to forgive others but was not able to forgive myself and that was a massive stumbling block that held me back in many areas.

- I had to learn to not walk around with the scarlet letter of "**S**" for shame on my heart and openly receive God's forgiveness.

📖 *Level* of **TRUST** | Proverbs 3:5 (NIV)

- o *Trust in the Lord with all your heart and lean not on your own understanding.*
  - Trust is a crucial element of faith and they go hand in hand.
  - Trusting God had become the hallmark of my life.
  - I had to learn to weigh every word that came through my ear gate and every observation that passed through my eye gate against the *Word of God*.

📖 *Nails* of **LOVE** | 1 John 4:8, 16 (NIV)

- o *God is **Love**.*
  - Jesus's love nailed Him to the cross for our sins, which is an inexpressible gift.
  - Jesus's love cleansed and washed me white as snow, which is an inexhaustible gift.
  - Jesus's love is free to all who believe, which is the ultimate indescribable gift.

📖 *Goggles* of **PEACE** | John 14:27 (NIV)

- o *Peace I leave with you; my peace I give you. I do not give to you as the world gives. Do not let your hearts be troubled and do not be afraid.*
  - I had to learn that peace is a precious present from the heart of God, wrapped in love.
  - I had to learn that peace is not the absence of chaos.
  - I was astounded when God showed me a peace that surpasses all understanding while amid a fiery storm brewing–an unforgettable moment etched upon my heart.

📖 *Joist Drill* of **JOY** | Nehemiah 8:10 (NIV)

- o *For the **joy** of the Lord is your strength.*
  - Joy is from the Lord and His joy gives us the strength to press on.

- I had to learn that difficult times cannot steal your joy when your joy is in God.
- Joy is the gift that God gives to us every day and we have to learn to walk in it. Joy and happiness may meet at the same crossroads but they are distinctly different. Happiness is what we feel as long as all is good. Joy is what we have in the good and bad. The joy in God is everlasting, whereas happiness can be fleeting.

📖 *Tape Measure* of **FAITH** | Romans 12:3 (NKJV)
- *God has dealt to each one a measure of faith.*
  - I learned that the measure of faith will be different for each person.
  - God's Word said that I only needed the size of a mustard seed (the smallest of tree seedlings). When I saw the mustard seed, I believed that I could have that size faith.
  - I was learning to keep the shield of faith up at all times and press forward.

📖 *Mallet* of **MERCY** | Lamentations 3:22–23 (HCSB)
- *Because of the LORD's faithful love we do not perish, for His mercies never end. They are new every morning; great is Your faithfulness!*
  - God's mercy **saved** all of us at the cross.
  - I had to learn to receive God's mercies daily.
  - I had to learn to extend to others the same mercy that I wanted for myself.

📖 *Bolt* of **PRAISE** & **WORSHIP** | Deuteronomy 10:21(BSB) & Psalms 95:6(HCSB)
- *He is your praise and He is your God, who has done for you these great and awesome wonders that your eyes have seen.*
- *Come, let us worship and bow down: let us kneel before the LORD our Maker.*
  - God is worthy of our praise and worship.
  - I learned that praise is a war song and worship is the war cry.

- I learned that praise and worship precede the victory battle.

📖 *Saw* of **SALVATION** | Acts 4:12 (NIV)

  o *. . . Salvation is found in no one else, for there is no other name under heaven given to mankind by which we must be saved.*

  - *Salvation* is free to all who would open their hearts to receive it, there is no cost to be saved!
  - Jesus Chris is the Savior and the Redeemer of the world.
  - I learned that genuine repentance leads to *Salvation* and for that I am grateful.

God had me on the Potter's wheel. He used each of these tools in the toolbox to chip away everything that was holding me back from being who He called me to be. It took me a while to sit still and be obedient because I kept trying to do it my way and He kept putting me back on the Potter's wheel; spinning, shaping, discarding, adding; spinning, shaping, discarding, adding—over and over and over again until I submitted to His will. I would love to say that this was a quick process, however; this has been years in the making. These priceless jewels were put into my toolbox little by little, day by day, month by month, and year by year to prepare me for such a time as this. God took me by the hand and allowed me to find His treasure chest of **gem**s that were instrumental in the toolbox for my character development. He s*haped* me on the Potter's wheel of love. He *replaced* my brokenness with His anointing hands. He *developed* my spiritual muscles. He *anchored* my heart to hope in Him. He *aligned* my soul to trust Him. He propelled me into my purpose. I do not leave home without my treasure box or tool chest. These items help me to remain in a posture to always be positioned to **War Up**.

God is a supernatural God who can do supernatural things. We have to allow the Holy Spirit to activate the God (Christ) within us. God can do anything. There is nothing impossible for God. There is nothing too hard for God. There is no foe that God cannot defeat. There is no conquest that God cannot conquer. There is no movement that God cannot stop. There is no battle waged against God that He cannot prevail. God is your battle fighter and all you need to do when you walk into your war zone is to remember who you are and whose you are. The battle was won when you took the first step in accepting Christ! Forward march into your destiny and purpose. **War Up**!

FORECAST

Cloudy overcast for most of the day. The beams of sun rays will peak through the clouds in spurts. There is an 80% chance of rain showers. I had better find my **War Up** boots. I don't want to step into any puddles of trickery on this journey.

---

*Gear up with the glory of God and **War Up** with the Word of God! Keep cadence with God's direction!*

9

Unexplainable Season

THE PUZZLEMENT

Many unexplainable things happened to me during this *Season* in the form of signs, wonders, and miracles. God used this *Season* to grow me up. My dependence on Him became my new posture. God was no longer an option but the air I breathed literally. I knew without a doubt that I had to jump one hundred percent into the safety of His Mighty arms, or I would not survive this Season. Thus, during this dark *Season*, I became very close to Him. The *Season* was very difficult to navigate. I clung to Him like a baby to a bottle. If it was not in *His Word*, I did not want to read it or see it. I was solely focused on sticking to God like glue and waiting in expectancy for my healing.

As I mentioned earlier, I had listed every healing Scripture or any Scripture that spoke to my spirit during this *Season*. I had about 25 healing Scriptures that I repeated daily in the Name of the Father, Son, and Holy Spirit. It was my medicine. My biblical Tylenol. I took it faithfully three times a day. Those Scriptures became the medicinal healing balm to my mind, body, and soul. Healing was not an option. I truly believed there was nothing that God could not do. I did not understand how He would do it, but I believed that He would do it.

I knew I had to do my part, which was to declare the *Word* out loud, believe the *Word*, and stand on the *Word* no matter the circumstance. I had to anchor my trust in God in this *Season*. I could not—would not waver. For me, the stakes were too high.

In this *Season*, I had to face many obstacles, mountains, and battles that were used to grow my spiritual muscles. The most important lesson for me at the time was learning how to trust in the reliability of the *Word of God*. Psalms 93:5 (CSB) states it like this: *Lord, Your testimonies are completely reliable; holiness adorns your house for all the days to come.* God's Word is reliable! It is up to us to trust what the Word says and to be in expectation to receive it. In this *Season*, I had to learn how to handle adversity and discern when to speak the *Word of God*. And to speak the *Word of God*; I had to know the *Word of God*. Thus, I was constantly in the **Bible**. The time was now for me to speak life over my situation and believe the impossible by faith. I hid the following Scriptures in my heart.

- *It is written:* (Romans 14:11 NIV).
- *So shall My word be that goes forth from My mouth;*
  It shall not return to Me void,
  But it shall accomplish what I please,
  And it shall prosper in the thing for which I sent it (Isaiah 55:11 NKJV).
- *God is not a man, that He should lie* (Numbers 23:19 ESV).
- *Life and death are in the power of the tongue* (Proverbs 18:21 HCSB).

On my journey towards healing, I had varying conversations with many people, some good and some bad. It has been my experience that people tend to give their opinions based on their understanding which when you think about it is a normal thing to do. Their understanding without the *Word of God* can become a stumbling block because they do not know what is written in *His Word*. It is critical that when the opinion of people move you to succumb to worry, doubt, or unbelief; it is at that point that you must check in with the Holy Spirit to validate what is true and what is false. Learning what to say helped me to stand firm and press into my faith. One of the Scriptures that spoke to me was: *All things are possible with God* (Mark 10:27 NIV). As far as what I understood, all meant all and therefore I stood on the belief that All things were possible, simply because: . . . *it is written:* (Romans 14:11 NIV). After all, that is what God had said and He could not lie.

I was learning to speak life over my circumstances, and I did just that even though the change was not present. This became a crucial lesson for me because there was no evidence of change. You mustn't allow people to take the pencil out of your hand to write their story onto your paper. The following are incidents where I had to snatch the pencil back out of the hand of these individuals and declare the *Word of God* over people's ill-will comments, opinions, and suggestions. Now, let me add a disclaimer. I honestly believe that the individuals in these scenarios did not mean any malicious intent and were coming from a place of their truth, their experience, and their reality. I just refused to accept their reality as my reality.

Scenarios

Scenario I
The doctor told me that I have a very aggressive cancer that had moved into my lymph nodes, but I will probably live for about five years.

But it is written: *I will not die but live*—Psalms 118:17 (NIV).

Scenario II
One day a visitor came by to ask why I thought I had breast cancer. I looked at her with bewilderment and said: "How would I know?" She proceeded to ask me question on harboring unforgiveness? She said:

> "A lot of times people get sick when they harbor unforgiveness."

The ironic thing is, I previously asked for forgiveness along with offering forgiveness to people who I knew I hurt and/or who have hurt me. If I had no way to reach the individual, I had written a letter seeking to be forgiven or forgiving someone who had done something to me. I thought this chapter of my life was closed. I told her this, she said:

> "Are you sure?"

Thus, I began second-guessing myself and guilt and condemnation came over me. She added:

> "You have breast cancer for a reason and you need to ask for forgiveness to make sure you are not harboring unforgiveness because that will make you sick."

People will sure put you in a fix if you are not aware of who you belong to. I spoke with my spiritual mentor because this issue was bothering me. She immediately took that thought into captivity and said:

> "Once you repented and asked for forgiveness then that was that. God has forgiven you and don't you believe anything other than that. Once you extend your forgiveness, the onus is on the person to accept it. You don't have to keep asking for His forgiveness—you're forgiven. Your sins were nailed to the cross."

But it is written: *We demolish arguments and every pretension that sets itself up against the knowledge of God, and we take captive every thought to make it obedient to Christ*—2 Corinthians 10:5 (NIV).

Scenario III

I had two people on my job who sounded like *parrots* of each other. I say this because it was as if they were having a conversation about me. This is how the conversation went. I will refer to the two people as *Parrot One* and *Parrot Two*.

Parrot One – How are you doing?
Myself – I am fine.
Parrot One – No really, how are you doing?
Myself – I am fine.
Parrot One – No, seriously, how are you doing?
Myself – I am fine.

Parrot One's Commentary: You can't be fine because my first wife died from the same thing.

****

Parrot Two – How are you doing?
Myself – I am fine.
Parrot Two – No really, how are you doing?
Myself – I am fine.
Parrot Two – No, seriously, how are you doing?
Myself – I am fine.
Parrot Two's Commentary: You can't be fine because my mother died from the same thing.

Believe it or not, these two people both approached me on the same day at different times. After the second parrot (person) approached me, fear attached itself to me like white on rice. I could not shake it. I became extremely somber and depressed. The only thing I could do was hurry to the bathroom and have a meltdown. I know that anyone who has cancer stands the possibility to die. However, I did not want to hear about how someone's wife died or how someone's mother died because we both had the same circumstances. I made a mental note to avoid these two parrots (people) should I ever see them coming my way again.

Again, let me reiterate, I don't believe that either one intentionally meant any malice towards me. I believe they wanted me to know their truths and the outcome of their situations, however; I refused to hold onto their demise. I had to lean into the hope of God since that was all I had at the time. My hope would carry me like a 747 on the wings of *His Word*. That is where I found refuge and peace. I discovered a Scripture that spoke to my spirit about only believing God. I held onto that Scripture and refused to let go. And I mean, I refused to let go. I took a page out of Jacob's story when he wrestled with the angel (Genesis 32:22–32) and he refused to let go. Jacob got a blessing when he did not let go and I believed that God would bless me if I did not let go as well. And let me tell you, I held on with a tight grip of belief and refuse to let go.

But it is written: *Do not fear, only believe*—Mark 5:36 (ESV).

Scenario IV

I was told that the chemotherapy would cause me to lose my hair, thus I would be bald. Just like the doctor said, I woke up with hair on my pillow and coming out in patches. This propelled me to shave off the rest of my hair or walk around with patches of holes all over my head. I went to the beauty supply store and began to entertain getting a wig. I liked the various wigs but none of them look good on me. Then the store attendant told me she could cut and style a wig for me. She did a great job. She styled my hair into a honey-brown bobbed wig. The wig was so hot, I do not know how people wear them. I only wore it outside of the house. Initially, I was going to have my natural hair made into a wig until they quoted me a price of approximately $900.00. I thought about that for a minute: $900.00 or $39.99 for the wig, well you guessed it, the wig won. I figured I could grow my hair back eventually after the treatment and I did.

But it is written: *For I have learned to be content whatever the circumstances*—Philippians 4:11 (NIV).

Scenario V

The type of chemotherapy that was prescribed for me rendered the side effects of paralysis. The paralysis was primarily in my feet and some in my hands as well. I was in excruciating pain and I had to force myself to move to walk. My feet hurt at the softest point of a touch. The agony of the pain in my feet was horrifying. One day while I was sitting down because my feet were hurting so bad; I instinctively began massaging them. This was not a feel-good message. It hurt but I just kept at it and I am not sure why. What I noticed was the more I massaged my foot, the pain began to subside. I got so excited and preceded to do the other foot as well. This became a daily routine. God had somehow given me the prompting to massage my foot. Now and again, the pain would return and I would make a point to massage the area and the pain would dissipate. But God, who gave me an unction that remedied the paralysis in my feet.

But it is written: *Call to me, and I will answer you; I will tell you wonderful and marvelous things that you know nothing about*—Jeremiah 33:3 (GNT).

Scenario VI

I read Dodie Osteen's book where she had a miraculous healing. She had terminal cancer and not much time to live. Her family decided together that she was healed, and they would treat her as such. In her book, she said to do one thing each day that you would not normally do until you are better. I never forgot that. Because of the paralysis, I had to drag my feet and it took forever for me to get from point A to point B. I could balance myself upright so I decided not to use a cane or a walker (**side note:** if I was unable to balance myself upright then I would have used a walker or a cane, and still believed for complete healing). I went to work, and no one expected me to come into the office. They told me not to worry about anything but to get better. Yet, I was determined to press my way there. That was the one thing I did differently, and it was extremely hard to do. It was an absolute struggle to get there. The people on my job were amazed that I even showed up. Nonetheless, I pressed. In addition, I could not wear closed-toe shoes or high-heels. My feet felt like little flat elephant feet. I wore slides during this *Season*. I believed with my heart that I would walk, wear high heels, and closed toes shoes again. By the grace of God, I believed and God showed up and delivered!

But it is written: *I press toward the goal*—Philippians 3:14 (NKJV).

Scenario VII

One day I and my paralytic legs went to radiation. Now, my mom did not know that I drove myself to radiation. Radiation was every single day (Monday – Friday) with no breaks and I was not about to ask her to drive thirty minutes every single day to my house to take me five minutes down the road to the Cancer Treatment Center (CTC) facility.

As she reads this book, she will find out this information. I told her that someone was taking me, but I had no one to take me so I drove myself. One day as I arrived at the treatment center, a staff member asked me:

"Where is your driver?"

I commented that I did not have a driver and that I was fine. I also told her that I lived close. She said:

"You know you should not be driving alone to this treatment center."

I said I know, but I do not have anyone to bring me and again I affirmed that I live close. She preceded to comment on how I was walking. She said:

"You should have a walker or a cane."

And I said again I am fine. She proceeded to comment further and said:

"You know that the chemotherapy may cause permanent damage to your feet. My aunt had cancer and she can no longer walk; she has been paralyzed for years."

I thought, here we go again with these naysayers and I became quickly irritated. With attitude in tow, I simply looked at her and said emphatically, "The devil is a liar; I will walk again." And all she could say was:

"I know that's right."

Again, I do not think she meant any harm. She was simply stating the facts about her aunt. It may have been a fact for her aunt, it was a non-receiving fact for me. I refused to receive that negative report over my life. The golden rule would have done well with this naysayer; if you don't have anything positive to say, don't say anything at all.

But it is written: *No weapon that is formed against you will succeed*— Isaiah 54:17 (NASB).

Scenario VIII

The same visitor came back to see me again and asked about what was I eating while I was undergoing treatment? I told her and she exclaimed:

"No, you need to be eating this and that."

So, she brought me this and that to eat. I had never seen this and that before in my life. I asked what was this and that? She had explained what this and that was; and said:

"Eat it, it is good for you."

I tasted it, but the truth be told, I could not eat this and that because I had no idea what this and that was nor had I ever seen this and that before. The taste and smell of this and that made me queasy. During this *Season*, I did have stringent food instructions such as no microwave food, only fresh fruits, and vegetables, except soup and crackers. And absolutely no junk food or caffeinated dark drinks. I was leery of her presumptions of my situation and I refused to believe her so I threw away this and that and believed that God would provide exactly what I needed which was the diet that the doctor prescribed for me (fresh fruits and vegetables). I did not need to be condemned nor feel guilty for not eating this and that. Her judgments were becoming daunting.

But it is written: *Let not the one who eats despise the one who abstains, and let not the one who abstains pass judgment on the one who eats, for God has welcomed him. Who are you to pass judgment on the servant of another?*— Romans 14:3-4 (ESV)?

Scenario IX

My radiation treatments were scheduled every single day except Saturday and Sunday. As I was nearing the end of radiation treatments, the radiologist team did not like how my skin was looking. The radiation left my flesh raw with no skin. It was seared, red, and open. They gave pause and wanted me to allow it time to heal some and then come back and finish the treatments. I was saddened because it was my last week of treatments. I was ready for this to be over. I told them I did not care about the burn and I would sign a waiver–I just want to be done. They looked at me like I was talking nonsensically in which I was. The technician responded:

> "Do you see how bad this looks? This is an open sore
> and we will do more damage, it needs to heal before we
> can proceed with the radiation. You need at least a layer
> of skin there."

They ignored me as it was the right thing to do. They prescribed a burn ointment that I would have to use. I had to stop the radiation treatment. I cried because I just wanted it to be over. I used the salve and prayed that the area would be healed enough to finish the treatments before the New Year came in since it was now December. All I could say was, won't He do it! God healed me enough so that I could finish the treatment in December . . . But GOD!

But it is written: *Heal me, O Lord, and I will be healed*—Jeremiah 17:14 (AMP).

Life deals disappointments and hurls unanticipated obstacles that we have to face. I have come to learn that all obstacles are disguised as opportunities. When you change your outlook, you change your perspective. The obstacle no longer exists in the same form, and it transitions from obstacle to opportunity. I realized that everything I was going through was an opportunity to see things from a different outlook. I read somewhere that:

"The storms of life will strip your soul bare for a healing."

There were so many layers that needed to be stripped before I could receive complete healing. I desired not only physical healing, but spiritual, and emotional healing as well.

Our obstacles, which can be our disappointments will come. It is wise to understand that when they come you will need to go through, under, over, or across. Press forward and believe that with Christ, the journey will ultimately be successful. When we press, prod, and push; we receive extra radiant blessings of health, hope, and healing. We have to remember to only believe the report of God, no matter what we feel, no matter what people say, and no matter the disappointments of life. Hannah Hunnard, author of *Hinds' Feet on High Places*, sums it up like this:

> "Evidently my Lord has something very important to teach me. And, oh! I do want to learn it. One thing I can do radiantly and gladly is: to go through each day praising for everything that happens. For the disappointments as well as for the joys. For disappointments accepted with praise always seem to turn into extra-radiant blessings!"

Disappointments Storms	Praise In midst of Storms	Extra-Radiant Blessings Balm in Gilead
Breast cancer	. . . even now You are Faithful	He healed me
Unforgiveness	. . . even now You are Merciful	He forgave me
Double attack	. . . even now You are Powerful	He protected me
Hair Loss	. . . even now You are Incredible	He provided a wig
Paralysis	. . . even now You are Miraculous	He remedied a cure
Impossible feat	. . . even now You are Victorious	He made the impossible possible
Disable gait	. . . even now You are Compassionate	He ordered my steps to walk
Guilty conscious	. . . even now You are Gracious	He removed guilt
Treatment setback	. . . even now You are Amazing	He favored my comeback

Cancer is an unwelcome entity in anyone's life. When you are in a dark place, it is important to hold onto the *Word of God*. The best antidote to places of darkness is praise. If you are praising, you cannot be complaining. Negativity and positivity cannot leap from your tongue at the same time. I believed that He would deliver me. I did not know how, but I believed that I would be completely healed. I also believed that God could help me with my unbelief and I stood on that Scripture as well: *I believe. Help my unbelief*—Mark 9:24 (NHEB).

Trusting God amid the storm when everything around you begs to differ was extremely difficult. I had done all that I knew to do. I felt wiped out many times and I wanted to give up. Stumbling blocks are inevitable. It is how you pick up the blocks that matter. We are all prone to miss the mark and make mistakes. But as a child of God, Christ will grab you by the hand and pick you back up again. His hand is there, hold on, and never let go.

══════════════ FORECAST ══════════════

The temperature will drastically drop below freezing;
however, a warm front will move in bringing a
high of 40 degrees with plenty of sunshine.

———⚬⚬⚬———

Turn on your trust-o-meter, God got you!

FALL EQUINOX
Climate, Change, and Colors

And let us not grow weary of doing good, for in due
Season we will reap, if we do not give up.
Galatians 6:9 (ESV)

The autumn hues in the *Fall* are beautifully eye-catching. The tones of coloration radiate beams of diversity. In this *Season*, change is evident, consistent, and ever-present. You become open and clear about what you should retain and what you need to let *Fall* off of you. You shake the leaves of fear, frustration, and foolishness, and you retain the trunk, branch, and sapling, which are the foundation of the tree. Let everything that serves no purpose *Fall* away. As one author stated:

"Autumn shows us how beautiful it is to let things go."

In this *Season* you reevaluate and consider what is important and what is not. You have to aerate the ground of hope, plant the seedlings of faith, and fertilize the soil with love. Just like any masterpiece, change is generally not an overnight process. The change will stretch and grow you up in spiritual matters. It is not easy but always worth it in the long run. Many times, the change is not only for you but for others around you.

Let God shape you to bring forth the purpose that He has instilled in you from your mother's womb. God has placed in us our talents, skills, love, education, hope, and much more. Until you activate your talent, skills, etc., you cannot grow into your best self. Many of us don't grow into our best selves because we are too busy mirroring everyone else. Marianne Williamson said:

> "Who am I to be brilliant, gorgeous, talented, and fabulous? Actually, who are you to not be, you are a child of God."

In this *Season* we have to allow God to shake the many leaves that are holding us back from the promises of God. We need to shake the leaves of frailties, insecurities, and frenemies; along with anything else that holds us back like the leaves of hopelessness, unfaithfulness and busyness. We need to take notice of the old leaves as they *Fall* to the ground and simply leave them there. Turn away and walk into a new *Season*.

The *Fall* brings change and it's vital to embrace the change. Let the colors of love, grace, and mercy *Fall* into your faith as you till the soil of your soul. Remember that when things are *Fall*ing down all around you, it is only because they are *Fall*ing into place.

FORECAST

The beauty of autumn unfolds within the barometric pressures on earth in bountiful hues. It's a beautiful thing when you can catch the colors of change as they ***Fall***!

—❦—

"Autumn . . . the year's last loveliest smile."
William Cullen Bryant (Town& Country Magazine)

10

Unyielding Season

THE PERSISTENCE

This book has been a long time coming. I started this book too many times to count. I just could not seem to get it done. I considered how I would write the book, what the title would be, and what I was going to expound upon. I wondered if the book would be autobiographical or written through a story tale (truth alongside an imaginary tale). One of my favorite books, *Hinds' Feet on High Places*, was written in this manner. The characters are animals, but the message is pure truth. I desire that this book would capture the essence of God. I wanted to capture every miracle, sign, and wonder that God had done for me in this *Season*. God had really done a lot of marvelous things in my life as a new believer. I was once told that God shows up and shows out for the new believers. I believe that because I truly experienced God showing up for me continuously when I first became **saved**.

My life was super busy with all kinds of stuff, activities, distractions, and work. I wanted to write the book, but I was being pulled in many different directions. Since I started this book, I was promoted on my job into a new series which brought new work that kept me very busy. I went back to school and obtained my Master's Degrees. I continuously did volunteer work. I was an active member of many non-profit organizations. My kids graduated from high school and went on to college. I was a mother, homemaker, resume writer, decorator, friend, neighbor, traveler, choir member, liturgical dancer—just to name a few. I was also active in my sorority and the Ladies' Ministry at my church. I attended conferences, local and outside of my state. I am sure that I have overlooked something, but you get the point. I liked having something to keep me busy. I was busy being busy but not necessarily beneficial busy for myself. When someone asked, I said yes. I could not say no. That was my biggest downfall. I needed to decide to simply say "no" with love. I made everyone's schedule a priority and allowed my purpose to drop to the wayside.

All of these things were good things, but I kept making myself available to others and not doing what I needed to do for myself, which was to walk into my purpose. I had to learn to make better decisions for myself. The decision to make a decision has always been a struggle for me. When I made a decision and if it ended up being a wrong decision, it left me not trusting the next decision that I would need to make. To make matters worse, I ponder too long over every decision. I am a salesman's greatest opportunity. If you come to my house with your product, consider it sold. It's later that I wish I did not purchase the item. And because of hesitating on a decision, many of my decisions were made for me by people who have taken it upon themselves; such as a salesman, to make the decision that I would not make.

The decision to decide or not to decide is still a decision. I have since learned that indecisiveness concerning a decision is a decision to live a chaotic lifestyle. There is a danger to haphazard decisions. Here I am in the fourth *Season* of my life since *Winter, Spring,* and *Summer* have passed. Now it is *Fall* and I need to change the colors of my direction. To write or not to write is a decision. I have decided to write. I believe I have just made a decision! Fingers, don't fail me now!

"Sometimes silence is so loud that it can deafen the ear lobes of the heart."
The soundless responses were noisily wringing alarms in my head. Sometimes I would hear from God and sometimes I would not. I was wondering why God was being uncommunicative now? And it always seemed to happen when I felt that I needed Him most. I kept crying out to God. Where are you? I am walking on the heels of a Maskil of the sons of Korah where Psalms 44:23-24 (HCSB) states: *Wake up, Lord! Why are you sleeping? Get up! Don't reject us forever! Why do You hide and forget our affliction and oppression?* I could not let go of this Psalm that spoke to my heart. It gave me a sense of calming knowing that others in the past had cried out with the same plea from their varying struggles in life. It seemed like my tears were being emptied into the cracked porcelain bowls within my soul.

The silence felt like a screaming rejection and it pierced my heart with sorrow.

My heart kept crying out to hear His voice. God, where are You? God, I need You! God, are you listening? I deeply sighed as my pain strum pain strummed to a noiseless beat of frustration. It seemed like God had left the scene and I did not know what to do. Yet, I knew what I needed to do.

Not hearing from God is difficult. The silence becomes a test of wills. Will I hold on to my beliefs about God or will I surrender to my emotions in defeat? God had answered me on numerous occasions, but it was like He had hit the mute button and gone completely silent. My faith was waning again and I struggled to keep it in check. I was exhausted from this on-going tug-of-war. I was perplexed as to how to go about this faith thing on a continuum basis because I didn't want to hit a high only to come crashing back down to a low. I was trying to have the faith the size of a mustard seed that the **Bible** talks about but I could not stop wavering.

In this *Season*, I felt very alone. It bothered me that I could not hear from God nor could I feel His presence. The only thing I could feel was the excruciating pain throughout my body from the chemotherapy treatments. I ached all over in the worst way. An eerie feeling of darkness was hovering over me. It seemed like everything was going from bad to worse. I peered at my nails (toes and hands) and I burst out crying when I saw them. They were black. It was a deadened black that appeared to have no life. This was also something that the doctor told me that would happen. Not only was I bald, but my fingernails and toenails had turned black, and the paralysis had kicked in full swing. My feet felt like they weighed a ton as I struggled to move them. The paralysis also affected my hands, thus; my very good handwriting was bordering on poor. I did not want to eat in front of people in fear of dropping the utensils. My hope was draining from me fast. I was tired of the struggle. I wanted so badly to hear from God. Yet, God seemed extremely quiet. It was like He completely left the stage, and I would have to get through this performance on my own.

I had so many questions. There was so much I did not understand. What do you do when you cannot hear the voice of God or feel the presence of God? God had delivered me on numerous occasions and had answered many of my prayer requests; some even instantaneously or before I could even utter the request. Yet, right now—He seemed to be M.IA. (missing in action). I could not help to wonder if it will always be like this. I found myself questioning God's methods. I knew that questioning God's method was futile, and I also knew what I needed to do. I needed to activate the measure of faith that He had given to me. Faith is believing when you have absolutely no reason to believe. I knew this statement to be true, so I decided to put my feet to my faith.

Standing on faith amid the storm is difficult because fear sets you up to fail. Fear is a polluted environment. I read a mnemonic that stated that fear is **False Evidence Appearing Real**. And the mnemonic for faith is **Forwarding All Issues To Heaven**. Fear and faith cannot coexist together. Your faith may look dreary, but your faith is what you need to move forward. Fear is a stumbling block and faith is an anchor. I knew I should not worry but I could not control the run-a-way thoughts in my head. I needed to release all my worries to God. I remembered the words from Corrie Ten Boom:

"Worry is a cycle of inefficient thoughts whirling around a center of fear."

Learning to cast all my worries upon God would take a lot of effort on my part but I pressed anyway. I knew that girding up my faith would help strengthen my spiritual muscles. It didn't matter where my belief-o-meter was set on, I tuned into the frequency of God to help me with my unbelief. I needed to stand firm, trust God, and anchor my hope in Him.

The one thing I did understand was that God was stretching me to rely on Him and Him alone. I began to delve even deeper into the **Bible**. I kept finding Scriptures that spoke to my spirit and for that, I was truly grateful because they gave me a semblance of hope. One day as I was reading the **Bible**, I had an *aha* moment. I realized that God was speaking to me in different ways. He was speaking to me through *His Word*, songs, prayers, books, sermons, etc., and I began to pay close attention.

To say that I am glad that I pressed into the presence of God even when I did not feel like it is an understatement. As I reflected on how I felt initially when I stopped hearing from God; it would have been a huge mistake to listen to my feelings and miss the opportunity to trust God. I sought God daily in *His Word* and He began to reveal things to me. It wasn't that God had stopped talking, He was talking to me differently. One day He spoke to me through *His Word*. He gave me a Scripture to speak to the cancer. God directed me to Hebrews 11:33-34 (NIV). God, in His loving-kindness stopped by and gave His daughter these specific Scriptures to pray over my situation. I was super appreciative and truly grateful. I could not stop thanking Him. Below is the Scripture that God gave to me to speak over my circumstance and how each line was directly answering the diagnosis.

Hebrews 11:33–34

Who through faith conquered kingdoms,
cancer kingdoms

Administered justice,
    The Word
And gained what was promised;
    healing
Who shut the mouths of lions,
    naysayers
Quenched the fury of the flames,
    chemo
And escaped the edge of the sword;
    radiation
Whose weakness was turned to strength;
    through Jesus Christ
Who became powerful in battle and routed foreign armies.
    hormone therapy

Once again, I had an instinctive knowledge of what each verse meant. I knew that this Scripture spoke to the cancer. I marveled at how God took the time to give to me a healing Scripture and the wherewithal to break the Scripture down. I spoke this Scripture over my situation three times a day in the name of the Father, Son, and Holy Spirit.

I was learning to anchor my sail (my faith) to God's port (the **Bible**). God was building my faith and trust during this *Season*. As I drew nearer to Christ, God revealed that healing bridges trust and trust propels His promises—for those who would wait on God and believe.

Psalms 119:105(ASV) says: *Thy word is a lamp unto my feet, And light unto my path.* God was showing me many things in the **Bible** that was already there but I had never seen before. It was as if He was illuminating the Word for me to obtain a deeper understanding. The **Bible** provided Pure Gold Bars of Wisdom, Precision Crystals of Enlightenment, Priceless GEMS of Knowledge, Pliable Metals of Discernment, and Precious Stones of Serenity. I could not get enough of the Word and I love that He took the time to point out everything that I would need on this particular journey. He was watching over me even when I did not realize it.

As parents, at times we watch our children from little ways off (not too close but not too far). God was always there, He was stretching my faith and watching me from a distance. Just as parents stand close enough to help their kids learn to walk or ride a bike, you know you have to get out of the way to let them try it alone. You are close enough to catch them when they fall down but hidden enough to watch them do it on their own. When they do it, you are their first cheerleaders and then they take another step, and another step, and so forth and so on. Even momma birds kick her birds out of the nest when she believes it is time for them to spread their wings and fly. The momma bird is there to catch them until they can catch their flight on their own. Likewise, I needed to spread my wings open wide to fly with complete trust in God. I had to believe that He would catch me and help me with my vulnerabilities before hitting the ground. This is how faith works, yet it was very hard for me to just take the first step to even spread my wings.

What I have come to learn is that when God is silent, He is growing our trust and stretching our faith. God is ever-present even through the silence. I was learning how to come into His presence even when I could not feel Him. He was watching over me and teaching me invaluable lessons of trust. He was waiting on me to trust Him completely.

=========================== **FORECAST** ===========================

Hot, humid, and muggy. Seek shelter indoors. The
sun will be scorching! Heed the warning and cover
yourself with SPF-50 Son screen for your refuge.

———∽∞∽———

Silence screams very loudly—can you hear those hushed whispers?

Unloved Season

THE PIERCING

No one knew that my heart's desire in this *Season* was to be around people. One individual told me later after everything was over that the reason she did not call or come around is that her mother told her to stay away from me during this *Season* of my life. I could not even respond to that comment. When a person is going through, just having someone to be with you for even five minutes is a blessing. It seemed that every time I told someone about the cancer, it was like I had the bubonic plague and they bolted. It is a true statement that words travel faster than the speed of lightning. So many people who I was supposedly close to fell away and that hurt me deeply.

Seasons come and *Seasons* go, and I had to learn that friends and family fell into the same category. Trying to make sense of everything was bothering me to the core. At my next appointment, I was talking to my doctor about my worries. What she said made me pause and reconsider my thoughts. She made the following statement:

> "In this *Season* it is extremely critical that you do not worry about anything. You can deal with all that later.

In this *Season* your only focus should be total peace for total healing. If you are worrying, you will do more damage to your body."

I took her words to heart and began to try to let go of everything bothering me from my house not being spic and span clean, laundry piling up, lack of visitors, friends aloof, just to name a few. I had to loosen my grip and cast my cares and worries upon God. At this juncture, I knew I needed Him more than ever now. I needed God's help to change my focus from the hurt and turn my total focus to healing.

Although I was hurt by the ones that faded to black, I would come to realize that God was doing something different in my life. The more people faded to black, the more my focal perspective was turned inward towards Him. I began to be intentional about focusing on the promises of God. I had a rudimentary knowledge of the **Bible**. I did not understand how everything falling apart could work in my best interest. I could not quite grasp that concept but I pressed into *His Word* anyway. As I fed on the *Word of God*, I began to glimpse slivers of hope.

The **Bible** was becoming my source of hope and my direct line to God. Even though I was reading about the promises of God; I was not seeing the results of the promise. It seemed like the more promises I wrote down, the worse my situation had gotten. There was a steady decline in my entire body. It did not seem like His promises were working. My flesh said, "not going to happen," but my heart said, "Trust God's promises." This was the tug-of-war that I had to struggle with on a continuum basis. If I had to surmise where my trust odometer read at the start of the chemotherapy, I would say my flesh would equal eight and God's promises would equal two. I felt like my flesh was winning and there was evidence to prove it. Having actual proof of every ailing ache in my body made it just that much harder to hold on to the promises of God. It was like I was reciting them but not believing them because I could not see the results. The evidence of the results was staring me right back in the face. It seemed like overnight I went from good to bad, whole to broken, no pain to massive pain, satisfied to dissatisfied, and normal to abnormal in an instance. I went from:

- Hair *to* bald
- Clear normal nails and toenails *to* black fingernails and toenails
- Walking *to* forcing myself to move my partially paralytic feet
- Steady hands *to* jittery painful hands
- Pain-free feet *to* painful feet at the slightest touch
- Taste buds *to* lingering disgusting taste in my mouth
- Energy *to* completely exhausted
- High heels *to* flat slip-on shoes (cannot put a normal shoe on either foot)
- Friend connections *to* barely any friend connections
- Socializing *to* non-socializing
- Working full time *to* working a portion of time (about 10% for the month)
- Driving 100% *to* only driving a portion of time (impacted by medication)
- Working in the yard *to* unable to work in the yard (sunlight caused edema)
- No tattoo marks *to* tattooed marks for radiation
- Able to raise left arm *to* unable to raise left arm (lymph node removal)
- Kneeling *to* unable to kneel (excruciating pain in knees and feet)
- Squatting *to* unable to squat (balance was off)

The list of what I could not do grew longer by the day. There kept being something continuously added daily to this list and it got quite depressing. I wanted my normalcy back. I wanted to go back to the way it was. Once I attempted to return to one of my normal routines, ignoring the doctor's orders and that turned disastrous. I went outside to work in my yard, even though I was told to keep away from direct sunlight. I was busy in my yard weeding, gardening, trimming back plants, etc. I do not remember how long I was outside when I happened to notice my arm and gasped in horror! Edema had quickly set in on my arm. My arm became so swollen that it looked like elephantiasis. I became scared to death. They said no sunlight and I did not listen. I hurried up and got away from the sun and ran into the house. I cried and began praying and massaging my arm. God, with His loving-kindness and mercy, healed me that same day. I wore a compression sleeve whenever I left the house from that day forward. I had learned my lesson and the edema never returned. I had to learn the importance of being obedient even though I desired otherwise.

I went from healthy to everything going haywire and falling apart in a flash. I could not grasp how to bring back normalcy into my world. I felt like the nursery rhyme Humpty Dumpty, who fell off the wall and could not be put back together again. I witnessed that as life circumstances advanced unexpectedly, they come like a whirlwind spinning out of control. I learned that you may fix it or replace it, but it will never get back to the original structure. My original unmarred structure was a body free from cancer and surgery. I thought I was in optimum health until my applecart got turned upside-down.

The biggest applecart that turned over was friends and family. It says a lot when friends and families who you anticipated supporting you during this plight, faded to black. Didn't people know that they spoke volumes in their silence or lack of presence? As my circle of friends and family trickled down; I had a lot of downtime to think. I began questioning what type of person I was that the majority of my family and friends would fade to black. This made me take a deeper look at myself.

This *Season* was very dark and bleak for me. In this mirk and mire of darkness, the burden of sadness constantly overwhelmed me. I needed to get a grip on myself because I felt like I was slipping into a deep depression. I searched the **Bible** for answers, but it just felt like the solutions were out of reach. I wondered if I was even worthy of the promises of God? I felt dejected!

The one thing that did remain constant was the blessings of my mother's presence. My mother brought light into my dark, horrid, and pessimistic world. My mother would see me crying and in pain and would simply say to me:

"And this too shall pass."

The moment I felt myself slipping into a deep dark depressive state; I would recall my mother's words to me, and they would give me a semblance of hope:

"And this too shall pass."

I thank God for my mother during this *Season*. Those five words that she uttered to me, meant more to me than she could ever imagine. I hung onto those words for dear life and they encouraged me to press forward. I am truly grateful beyond words to have her for my mother. She is the epitome of a mom who exhibited true unconditional love.

To say that I felt unloved in this *Season* is an understatement. I expected God to know what I needed. I thought He understood that I needed to be hugged. I needed to have some friends. I needed my extended family. I needed to feel some semblance of love. Initially, I thought; maybe, I am a bad person. Actions do speak louder than words. Let me be clear, I did receive some calls and cards, which lifted my spirits tremendously, but only a handful of visitors. This bothered me initially until I remembered Romans 8:28 (NET): *And we know that all things work together for good for those who love God.* Somehow, I had to believe that everything was happening the way it was supposed to be happening for a reason.

Even amid the muck and mire, my heart's desire was to press into authentically seeking Him. As I sought God wholeheartedly, I asked Him to align my heart with His heart. I did not want any hidden agendas in my heart that would be contrary to His will for my life. Although many doors that were previously opened were shut, that did not deter me from putting my hope in Him. I did not understand Him, but I was learning to trust Him as I leaned on His promises.

His promises were not evident initially. Thus, the shroud of darkness would leave me feeling despondent at times. It was difficult to believe that God was with me, because my world was falling apart all around me. I felt leprous. It was like I had a plague and if someone got too close to me, they would catch the disease as if it was transferrable like a common cold. It felt like everyone had turned their backs on me. I was in tormenting pain mentally and physically. The pain just lingered like an irritating eyelash on your eyeball that you struggle to get out. And once the eyelash is out, relief comes. Yet, I could not find relief. The anguish, pain, and frustration drove up and parked themselves on the corner of my mind and put the emergency brake on—they simply would not go away. They were the thorns in my side that I could not break free from and it was testing my last ounce of strength. My mind was very hazy and confused. I hated the pitiful feeling of being discouraged.

One day I decided to read about healing stories that a friend had given to me. I perked up as I began to read about many miraculous healings. My frequency was now tuned into healing stories from anywhere—the **Bible**, people, books, music, TV, etc. I had read and heard about so many different types of healings, even about limbs being restored and that gave me a new wind of encouragement. I was so hungry for healing that I collected, researched, and inquired about anyone's healing. As I soaked in all the wonderful healing stories, I realized that everyone had a common theme, they did not waver. Because I sought to heal so bad, I reasoned that if God could heal them, then He could heal me. I did not care how He would heal me, whether it was instantaneously or through medicine—I simply wanted to be healed. I began to believe that *nothing is impossible for God* (Luke 1:37—CEV) not even the limb story. After all, He healed a limb in the **Bible**, so why could He not do the same thing today: *Jesus, the Messiah, is the same yesterday and today—and forever* (Hebrews 13:8—ISV). And if the Word was true yesterday, then it certainly had to be true today.

I can remember attending my first Women's Conference with Ebenezer AME (African American Episcopalian) Church. The conference was being held at the Marriott in Washington, DC. During this conference there was a specified time for prayer and the laying of hands for healing. I desperately wanted to attend. Somehow, I got the times wrong and had missed the session. I became distraught and began to cry because I wanted to receive a healing touch. The lady understanding my urgency told me to hold on and she went to look for the *Woman of God* to lay-hands on me. The *Woman of God* began praying for me beginning at my head and moving down my body. When she got to my stomach, I felt something go off in my stomach, like an explosion—POW. This is the best that I can explain this scenario. The POW was so strong that both of us fell back. I was told this information by my friends who picked me up. I did not know or even understand what happened. As I reflected on this later, I truly believed that a stronghold of some sort was broken, loosed, or freed; even though at the time it was unbeknownst to me.

I took a hold of those healing stories and events and held them close to my heart. I tied each one to a healing Scripture so that when the enemy decided to pounce, I could quickly respond with the medicinal pre-Scriptures (prescription) as a defense. Although it may seem as if I was prepared, nothing can prepare you like real-time experience. Too many times to count, I would waver, cry, doubt, sulk, and hang from anything negative. As His promises began to kick in, and I was learning to take a hold of those negative thoughts and replace them with the *Word of God*.

God in all His wisdom understood what I needed most and that was to be in His presence. God loved me that much that He had me all to Himself. He had my full attention. And since He had me all to Himself, He could shape me and grow me as He deemed necessary. He knew I was like a caterpillar in a cocoon striving to break free from my own personal chrysalis. Being in the cocoon can be a very dark place. In this dark place, you will learn to trust God; thus, bud and blossom or succumb to distress (worry and anxiety) and be defeated.

Like the butterfly, if any outside influences try to help the caterpillar, you end up crippling the butterfly for life. God allowed everyone to fall away so that I would not become crippled. The caterpillar depends on what God has already instilled in itself. I had to allow God to show me what He had already instilled in me. I desired to emerge as a butterfly, but I had to learn to surrender to the will of God while He was developing me in the chrysalis. God was remaking, reshaping, and rebuilding me anew. Just like 2 Corinthians 5:17 (NLT) states: . . . *anyone who belongs to Christ has become a new person. The old life is gone; a new life has begun!*

Learning to surrender to God had been one of the hardest lessons I have had to learn because it required completely letting go and completely trusting all matters to Him. Corrie Ten Boom says it like this:

"When I try, I fail. When I trust, He succeeds."

Trusting God opens your heart to unlock many blessings. These blessings are for your benefit: *When the Lord blesses you with riches, you have nothing to regret*—Proverbs 10:22 (CEV). God, once again in His loving-kindness unlocked the following blessing in my life.

- Relationship | Awakening spiritually to the love of God
- Generosity | Giving time, treasures, and talents to partner with God
- Selflessness | Humbling and knowing it is all about God
- Discernment | Looking with fresh new eyes, through the lens of God
- Devotion | Dedicating precious quiet moments with God
- Worship | Touching the heart of God through songs
- Praise | Admiring God through songs, journaling, and prayer

I sought God daily and one of the reveals that came to me was the truth of what I was truly seeking. Initially, I realized that I was only seeking a healing primarily, but not necessarily seeking God wholeheartedly. I was still walking in the lane of WIIFM (what's in it for me). That was my entire focus, but God who shows mercy and compassion helped to shift my focus from what He could do for me to what I needed to do as His daughter for Him. And as His daughter; there was only one thing needed, and that one thing was to sit at the feet of Jesus and put my entire focus on Him. Our relationship gave me the hope and encouragement to press forward inside this dismal *Season*.

- I pressed past the statistics.
- I pressed no matter what I felt like.
- I pressed when I did not understand.
- I pressed through the pain and turmoil.

- I pressed through the emotions and tears.
- I pressed regardless of the voices of naysayers.
- I pressed past the point of people's stares and pity.
- I pressed no matter what thoughts entered my head.
- I pressed regardless of the doctor's factual diagnosis.
- I pressed when I could not see a light at the end of the tunnel.
- I pressed and fought every battle uphill and would not back down.
- I pressed and pressed until I had impressed God's Word on my heart. That pressing built up a fire that was kindled by His love:
  - I built up my spiritual muscles with the Armor of God (Ephesians 6:10-18).
  - I built up my spiritual heart muscles with the Love of God (1 Corinthians 13:4-8; 1 John 4:8, 16).
  - I built up my spiritual brain muscles with the *Word of God*. (Proverbs 30:5)

The more I pressed into the *Word of God*, the more I was building up my trust in God. I thanked God for building up my spiritual muscles for offense and defense to always be ready to **War Up**. I thank God for building up my spiritual heart muscles to a love that was too inexpressible to understand, yet perfectly beautiful to embrace. I thanked God for building up my spiritual brain muscles to the knowledge and wisdom of God.

I recalled a conversation I once had with this lady about my plight and I never forgot it. She said:

> "You are walking this journey because God knows you are strong enough to handle this plight. Many of times the plight is assigned to the ones who can carry the task so that they may be able to help someone else when they go through the same situation. Everything is not always about you, and this instance is no different. God is holding your hand and He will not leave you nor forsake you. God gave to you a vision that came directly from

Him. He showed you how you would be healed and what medications to take. That in itself is a miracle and a major blessing. Do you know how many people would love to have that blessing? God had already answered you from the onset of the crux of the diagnosis. You keep searching for healing that God already promised to give to you. You already have the answer that you keep seeking. You only need to believe that what He told you would come to pass."

Amazingly, oftentimes people will speak into your life, but because of how big your storm is, you can forget everything else and put all your energy into worrying and fretting. God is the beacon of light in a storm. He is the ray of light that beams through the clouds after a storm. Your faith has to be diligent no matter what the circumstances look like. Your faith is tested while you are in the storm. You have to praise Him in the middle of the storm and anchor your sails of hope upon Christ as you learn to build upon your faith.

God was schooling me on faith. I remembered that I only needed faith the size of a mustard seed. Henry Ford said:

"Whether you think you can, or you think you can't— you're right."

I had made up my mind, that I can, could, and would be healed. My understanding did not matter. I knew I had to believe, and I asked God to help me with my unbelief. I once read that:

"Faith is the bridge between where I am and the place God is taking me" (Shiva Neekum Shukla).

Your healing bridges trust and your trust propels the promises of God. I had to believe that the promises of God could cross the bridge to my impending healing. I did not care that it looked impossible.

A speaker's commentary on the word impossible had me thinking differently.

> "The word 'Impossible' can read—I'm Possible—simply by adding an apostrophe after the letter "I" and a space after the letter "M."

I like that: *Nothing is impossible for God* (Luke 1:37 CEV). I like that there are no limitations that anyone can put on God. I like that I can stretch my imagination to imagine the unimaginable. I like that His Mighty acts are incredible. I love that God produces the unbelievable. I love that the mind of God renders the unthinkable. I love that the **Bible** brings forth the inconceivable. I love that the promises of God are inexpressible. I love that God gave Jesus to me as the most precious gift which is inexplicably indescribable!

I believed that God was taking me somewhere. I believed that God had a purpose for me. I believed that this was my journey for this specific moment. I believe that God was walking alongside me. I believed that trust was not an option. I believed that the Word was my sword. I believed that hope was my anchor even when I could not see the sails because of the storm. I believed the pains were there to develop my character. I believed the Scriptures and love it when they walk right off the pages. I believed that everything would be restored by the grace of God. I believed that I would write about this experience and live to tell it. I believe! I believe! I believe! Yes, I truly believe God!

In this *Season*, I was asking God to give me favor especially since *His Word* said: *His favor is for a lifetime*—Psalms 30:5 (AMP). What I would come to learn is that God's favor does not necessarily look the way we expect it to look. God in His infamous wisdom always had my best interest at heart. And because God knew what was best for me, He may not have granted all of my requests. The one request that He did not grant was to make this cancer diagnosis go away. I did not want to deal with this, and I cried for days and months. The more I cried, it seemed like the worse the symptoms got. But God, who placed many angels amidst these brewing storms. I am grateful for every angel that

He placed in my life. God was shaping me and molding me for His purpose. God knew exactly what I needed and at the precise time that I needed it and then and only then did He provide it.

<hr>

FORECAST

The torrential winds are not allowing the aircraft to rise to the appropriate altimeter for the flight of faith. Because of the low visibility and cloud height, the pilot will need to reroute and change the course to land on the belief runway at Heaven's airport.

<hr>

In a dormant Season, when nothing is seemingly changing, breathe—selah—God is still faithful!

Unprecedented Season

THE PROMISE

I sense worship inside of me brimming over at the edges of my heart. I am so full that I cannot hold it back! My five senses had taken a temporary leave of absence, but God restored them to their normalcy. I sense the excitement reverberating in the depths of my soul. Echoing the sounds of *Life* and strumming to the beat of grace and mercy!

Can you *hear* that?
> Dogs barking, birds singing, bees buzzing, and rustling sounds of dry leaves

Can you *see* that?
> Stars shining, flowers blooming, moon glowing, and blue cumulous free skies.

Can you *feel* that?
> Snowflakes, raindrops, sun beaming, and cool breeze.

Can you *taste* that?
> Passion fruit, sweet strawberries, flavorful blueberries, and delicious pears.

Can you *smell* that?

Aaaaah, the sweet aroma of Life . . . and it smells good!

The following words gave me a sense of relief and a hope of restoration by my Oncologist:

> "You have completed your last treatments. And the additional good news is that you will not need to take hormone therapy. However, as a preventative, you will need to be on medication for the next ten years."

I was ever so happy to hear those words. I was done, finish, kaput! No more chemotherapy or radiation. This moment had blessed me tremendously. My Oncologist informed me that I would still have to come back every six months until told otherwise for follow-up appointments with her (oncologist) and the surgeon. Additionally, she added that:

> "Your body will return to normal, but it will take some time. The treatment killed as many good cells as bad cells. Allow your body the necessary time to become fully restored and remember, no stress."

I knew that only God could fully restore my health. On this journey, God became my refuge and strength. I leaned heavily on Him as I continued to wholeheartedly seek Him. Unbeknownst to me, while in my pursuit of seeking God, a beautiful relationship blossomed between us. What I realized was that the most important intent was not to write *a story* but to write on the tablet of my heart **the story**!

- **The story** of doubt to belief.
- **The story** of trials to triumphs.
- **The story** of a vision healing from God.
- **The story** of hopelessness to hopefulness.
- **The story** of miracles, signs, and wonders.
- **The story** of fearing mountains and facing giants.

- **The story** of God's ever-present hand in times of trouble.
- **The story** of how my relationship with God grew monumentally.
- **The story** that God is the same today, yesterday, tomorrow, and forever!
- **The story** of the girl who could not but the God who could and the God who did!

Along this journey, I had come to learn that the battle was never mine, but God's. In the scriptures, many battles were won because God was sought first. This tells me that the battle is first won as we humbly and sincerely submit to God with our petitions and prayers. It does not mean that there will not be any trials but it does mean that the trials will not control you.

I was amazed at the many biblical stories where the people of God did very little, yet they were victorious by the hand of God. Like when God had confused the enemy and they fought each other, that is nothing short of amazing. Or how David used one rock with his first slingshot that would instantaneously kill a giant. Or when God said, you won't have to fight, just shout, say what? Just shout! With power-packed results like this, who would not want God on their side?

God was ever-present during my darkest moments. I remembered a quote from Corrie Ten Boom that says:

> "No pit is so deep that He is not deeper still; with Jesus, even in our darkest moments the best remains, and the very best is yet to be."

I cosigned on this quote knowing that God would have the best for me. God had used this *Season* to build my spiritual muscles and strengthen my faith. I can recall the Scripture that says: *I gave you milk, not solid food, for you were not yet ready for it*—1 Corinthians 3:2 (NIV). If I had written this book fifteen years ago, the product would have been completely different because I was in a different mindset. My initial mindset was focused on blaming and complaining, that which served a self-purpose. But God who transformed me and renewed my mind, helped me to switch from a me-focus (blaming and complaining) to a He-focus (worshiping and praising).

The most priceless gift that God taught me was to meditate on *His Word*. The more I meditated on *His Word*, the more I wanted to be in *His Word*. Having God's Word close to my heart ignited a spark, that kindled a fire, that burst into burning flames: *His Word is in my heart like a fire, a fire shut up in my bones*—Jeremiah 20:9 (NIV). His love beckons us to come to Him and He always has an open arm of grace.

I truly love the grace of God. And I am amazed how He knows what is really in our hearts. I had so many questions that were more accusatory as opposed to me humbly asking. I love that God knew the truth of my heart. I love that God loved me enough to grow me in the dark places where I drew closer to Him. I love that God used my mistakes to develop me. I love that God saw through my fears and tears. I love that God was my refuge and He never left me. I love that God placed everything and everyone in my life for a reason and a *Season*. I love that God was teaching me how to pray. I love that God held my hand tightly and did not let go. I love that God loved me. I fell in love with God. I wrote Him a poem, simply because I love Him!

Ode to Abba Father

I love You Abba Father,
And I always will,
I am blessed to be your daughter,
Your grace and mercy I feel;

I love You Heavenly Father,
Creator of Heaven and Earth,
You are the source of power,
The One that gave me birth;

I love You wonderful Father,
For revealing Your hidden treasure,
Through the Bible for all to prosper,
Your beauty and glory without measure;

I love You precious Father,
Your grace refreshes my soul,
I love Your heartbeat in Scripture,
Your Word makes me whole;

Your Word makes me whole,
I love You Lord!
Your Word makes me whole,
I adore You Lord!
Your Word makes me whole,
I worship You Lord!

You are the heartbeat of my soul!
I love you Lord!

God's love cannot be fully explained, but it can be fully realized. It is so far beyond comprehension, yet it can be felt in the heart, mind, body, and soul. His indescribable work on the cross is nonsense to the unbeliever, yet it makes all the difference in the world to the believer. To know that no matter what you did or said, you are still loved and can be forgiven for the unthinkable—it can only be summed up in one word, LOVE! I gleaned this statement that spoke to my heart:

> "I may not understand everything, and I may not even appreciate all that I am going through or have gone through, or have experienced or will experience, but what I appreciate more than anything is how everything unfolds, it always unfolds with love."

God's love sent two beautiful angels (Rochelle and Lavern) to pamper me at the end of my chemotherapy treatments. These two beautiful women came and picked me up one day to take me out to lunch. On the way, we stopped at a Spa. I did not think much of it, because Rochelle is an elite businesswoman who owns her Salon (Sirod's). I assumed she was transacting business concerning her own business. When they called my name because there are millions of Lisa's in the world, I didn't think they were talking to me. Then Lavern said they are calling you. I was floored. If I had a mic, it would have dropped at that very moment. It was one of the most beautiful gifts that these two women could have given to me at that time. After suffering for months and struggling with the after-effects of the chemotherapy, I welcomed a moment of true relaxation. They treated me to a full-body massage spa day inclusive of a meal. I never anticipated nor saw this coming. Yet, God knew what I needed and when I needed it. Their kindness meant everything to me and for that, I am truly grateful. Their act of kindness gave me so much joy in my heart that words cannot begin to express my heartfelt appreciation. Being in a dark place for months and having two Sistah girlfriends bless me with a package of love, touched me to the core of my soul. I truly thanked my Sistah girlfriends from the bottom of my heart for this beautiful, unexpected blessing. I thank God for placing these two beautiful Sistahs in my life.

As if the spa-day package was not enough, my girlfriend Lavern had moved out of state and told me she was giving me a *life celebration party* as soon as my final treatments were over. When Lavern said she was giving me a party, I honestly did not know what to expect. I assumed it would be dinner with her immediate family with a celebration cake. I never fathomed a literal party with people who were sincerely happy for me and who did not know me. I had never experienced this type of love or support from people whom I have never met. This act of kindness blessed me beyond words. The way God used Lavern to bless me, made me want to in turn be a blessing to others. At my celebration, there was a songster, music, poetry, cake, balloons, and gifts. To say that I was speechless would be an understatement. I know she did this out of the kindness of her heart and did not expect anything in return, however; I want to give her a shout-out in this book. I thank God that He placed this beautiful *Woman of God* in my life. This poem is written with love and appreciation to Lavern, my Sistah girlfriend!

Ode to Lavern

Lavern, from the bottom of my heart,
To the tips of my soul,
Your friendship from the start,
Has encouraged me to grow;

You would always say to me,
You need to know who you are,
You would utter again to me,
And whose you are;

You have a beautiful spirit,
And not one to aimlessly chit-chat,
Your robust laughter—I can hear it,
As we talk about this and that.

You talked about God like He was your friend;
And He was,
You talked about God like You and Him had a personal
relationship;
And You do,
You talked about God like He was near;
And He was,
You talked about God like you believed Him;
And You did,

You blessed me beyond words,
With your friendship and kindness,
Your gift was like a songbird,
Singing celebrations of love and muchness.

Words cannot utter my appreciation,
and gratefulness of your friendship!

Before 2005, I did not understand or even know what a personal relationship with God was. I thought I had a relationship with God until I realized that I did not. I knew of Him, but I did not know Him. I thank God that He held my hand and did not let go amid blistery conditions in the *Winter Season*. I thank God that He watered and refreshed my soul with dewdrops in the *Spring Season*. I thank God that He kissed my face with rays of the sun and gave me hope in the *Summer Season*. I thank God that He opened the windows of my soul where He deposited His promises and fulfilled them in the *Fall Season*. Mostly, I thank God for the breath of life throughout every *Season!*

FORECAST

The sun is shining brightly, the blue skies reflect peace.
The temperature will be in the high 70s and go to
the low 60s. Love and healing will twinkle under the
stars that dance and clap with radiant sparkles.

God's ever-present love awaits us all!

Season endings

'Twas the Unforgettable Seasons of Promise!

WINTER CAST

Unleashed Season

FREEDOM

On this powerful journey, I learned the art of release and surrender in the *Winter Season*. I learned to shake loose things that were holding me back from becoming my best self. I learned that you will either speak life over your circumstances or death, but not both. I learned that speaking life was the most powerful and the most impactful resource that I had in my arsenal. I learned that negativity and positivity were opposites and that you cannot entertain both of them at the same time. I learned that when negativity wanted to take the wheel and drive my thoughts, I had to put on the brakes, pull over to the curbside, open the passenger door, kick negativity out, and double-click the locks. I learned to pick up gratitude, encouragement, and positivity. I learned that the choice was mine and I could control who dwelled in my headspace. I learned to take captive dejected and derogatory thoughts and replace them with the promises of God. The promises of God are Yes and Amen! As children of God, we need to know what His promises entail. There is nothing that God cannot do or will not do for His children as long as it aligns with His will.

I once saw a picture of a little child being fed Scriptures with a spoon. The parent was feeding the child with the *Word of God*. That picture resonated with me and I began to see the Scriptures as medicinal healing. I realized the importance of feeding oneself biblical truths for spiritual nourishment to become healthy and whole. I began taking daily doses of biblical pre-Scripture (prescription) to strengthen my inner-being and to develop my spiritual muscles. I believed God! I believed *His Word*! I believed His promises! I had one mission and one mission only and that was to hold onto the promises of God for complete healing.

God is a healer. You have to believe in the healing. You mustn't waver. God will be with you in the storm just as He was with the three Hebrew boys in the fire. He did not allow the fire to consume them. I had to believe that He would not allow the chemotherapy red fire to consume me. God will use the scars of the fire (pain, hurt, frustration) as a conduit to help someone else on the same path. I had to believe that my testing would become my testimony. It was the various testimonies from various people's stories that gave me the courage and strength to press forward and to let go of my doubts, worries, and fear.

Worry, doubt, and fear can be burdensome weights to carry. Releasing these burdensome weights over to God brings a sweet calming peace even amid a storm. Peace does not mean that there is no storm, it simply means the storm does not have you. I was in the storm but I was not alone because God's peace was present. God had me specifically in this *Season* for a reason. It was my *Season* to be trimmed, pruned, shaped, and molded for His purpose. All of these things were needed for my growth and development. God walked with me, held my hand, and did not let go. God's grace was with me throughout the *Winter Season*.

═══════════ WINTER CAST ═══════════

Just because we cannot feel Him, does not mean He is not present.
He is our ever-present help and our beautiful majestic Savior!
Winter snowcaps are beautiful skiing sites. It's a wonderful thing to ski the slopes to freedom through the promise of surrender!

SPRING CAST

Unlimited Season

FAVOR

Favor is from the hand of God. Favor does not necessarily look the way we assume it should look. Favor can be obvious, but many times it is blind to the human eye when looking from a spiritually impaired retina.

In the *Spring Season*, I had an unlimited amount of favor. Everywhere I turned, God was showing up and showing out in ways I could never imagine. He spoke to me a lot through *His Word* on countless occasions. There were also what I call hidden favors because they come as a result of our faith and beliefs. Favor is an outcome of God's mighty hand. There is no limit to God's favor. Sometimes what we think of as misfortune is actually favor. Favor is what we need and not necessarily what we want, however; it can be.

I did not want the breast cancer diagnosis and I could not see God's hand in that situation, let alone His favor. I wanted the favor for the diagnosis to be a misread. Yet, that did not happen. The favor was not just the healing vision, but that God would walk with me in the fire just as He did with the three Hebrew boys. Having the favor of God's hand with me could not be measured but it could be felt.

The **Bible** says: *You will have suffering in this world . . . I have conquered the world*—John 16:33 (HCSB). Suffering is an inevitable part of this world whether it is a headache, injury, splinter, disease, or any other ailments. The capacity of suffering is different, but the favor of God is the same. He is right there to walk with us through any storm. The **Bible** affirms this in Jeremiah 32:17 (ERV): *Lord GOD, with your great power you made the earth and the sky. There is nothing too hard for you to do.* After all: *. . . His favor lasts a lifetime*—Psalms 30:5 (NIV). The day God stooped down to show me how I would be healed was the most precious day of my life. God is a God that cannot lie. God's Word is incorruptible. That was the sweetest most powerful favor that He had ever bestowed upon me.

Back Road Vision

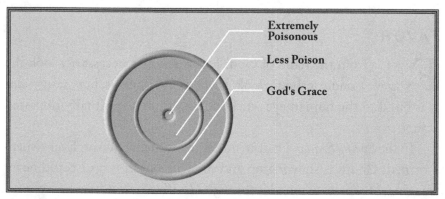

The planets are aligned and God has spoken, the stars will explode with a vision of healing.
Telescope viewing from an observatory brings forth discoveries. Discovering a one-on-one relationship with God will kindle flames of hope, trust, and love!

SUMMER CAST
Unveiling Season

FAITH

Faith took on a whole new level in the *Summer Season* because it required me to believe in something that I could not see. Trying to turn your focus over to positive thoughts while in excruciating pain turned out to be a massive struggle. God knows our level of faith and all He requires of us is to have faith the size of a mustard seed. When I first saw how tiny the mustard seed was, I believed that I could have that size faith. The mustard seed is super-small like the head of a straight pin but narrower. I could not believe that the tiny mustard seed I saw could grow to become a strong sturdy plant about eight feet tall. My faith needed to grow up and believe what was possible even without evidence. I needed to exhibit faith even when I could not see even the remotest possibility of its existence. Thus, I took words right off the author's page and adapted them to my scenario:

> "Faith is like radar that sees through the fog, the reality
> of things at a distance—that the human eye cannot see"
> (Corrie Ten Boom).

On this journey, it was critical that all of my pathways of open gates be tuned into the frequency of God. I found God mostly in *His Word* as I diligently sought Him. I kept my focus on Him. The *Summer Season* was all about me being closely connected to God, especially since the fire was burning out of control. If it was not about God; I was not interested. I was very guarded, like a fierce lioness with what went into my gate portals of my soul.

- **Ear gate** | I only allowed gospel and praise and worship music into my ear gate! I played Martha Munizzi's, CD continuously: *The Best is Yet to Come* spoke a healing balm over my situations and drew me very close to God.
- **Eye gate** | I could not get enough of the **Bible**. I thirsted for the *Word of God*. I read the **Bible** daily, it was not an option. The **Bible** was how I connected to God and one of the avenues of how God spoke to me.
- **Heart gate** | God would send many people on a continuum basis to give to me heartfelt messages, books, or sermons. Each of these methods touched my heart because they were all direct answers that I had inquired with God about. God provided exactly what my heart needed.
- **Tongue gate** | I had to learn to speak life and not fret over what I could not control. I had to speak life into those things that looked dead: *As it is written . . . the God who gives life to the dead and calls into being things that were not*—Romans 4:17 (NIV). If I wanted to see the opposite, I had to speak the opposite. I also had to ask God to *help my unbelief*—Mark 9:24 (WEB).

God wanted me to operate in faith whether I wanted to or not. It has nothing to do with feelings. He wanted me to trust in Him and only Him. *His Word* states in Hebrews 11:1 (KJV): *Now faith is the substance of things hoped for, the evidence of things not seen.* And in Hebrews 11:6 (NIV): *And without faith it is impossible to please God, because anyone who comes to Him must believe that He exists and that He rewards those who earnestly seek Him.* I was earnestly seeking Him with all my heart. My desire to be upright led me to incorporate the following as daily prayer request:

- Lord, help me to walk upright with You!
- Operate in my best interest, even when I do not like the answer!
- Continue to show me - - me!
- Teach me to love you when I do not like the outcome!
- Touch my heart and align it with Your heart!
- Let Your light shine through me that others may see You in me!

Faith can be a difficult walk because it requires you not to waver. Wavering is unbelief parked on a wishy-washy lane. Trying to stay on the straight and narrow road of belief is challenging: *but with God all things are possible*—Matthew 19:26 (NIV).

══════════════ SUMMER CAST ══════════════

Set sails of belief, anchors of hope, nets of love, and reels of peace!
**The sun from the *Summer* heat can burn. Block
the sun rays but don't block the Son days!**

FALL CAST

Unstoppable Season

FULFILLMENT

One of the most fulfilling things in life is when you press towards a goal and achieve the mark. I pressed toward the promise of God and received a healing. For that, I give God all the glory, honor, and praise. This journey was tough and although I did not want to take this route, I have to say that this route propelled me into having a deeper relationship with God. This journey drove me straight into His loving arms and for that, I am eternally grateful.

In God's loving arms, I learned that He is my Abba Father, my Dad, the Most-High God. I reverenced God and although some people feel like you dumb down God when you call Him Dad, it made me feel very close to Him. The dynamics of seeing God as the Father of creation and a personal Father only helped to deepen our connection; hence, the development of a personal relationship with Him.

A personal relationship with God will change you from the inside out. The personal relationship will take your stony heart that is filled with pride and ego and smash those hideous objects into smithereens. The personal relationship taught me to trust God and to look from His view and not my selfish judgments. Having a personal relationship with God showed me that every opposition is an opportunity to trust Him.

Just like the leaves on the tree change, God changed me. The leaves of disbelief fell, the leaves of bitterness fell, the leaves of anger fell, the leaves of hopelessness fell, the leaves of disparity fell, the leaves of envy fell, and the leaves of scarcity fell to the ground. But just as they fell, I too fell onto the ground. I fell onto my knees with lifted hands to worship God who is worthy of our praise and so much more!

FALL CAST

In the Fall, I fell, and I fell hard. All I can say is that falling in love with Jesus has been the best thing that has ever happened to me!

Fall into worship! Fall into Praise! Fall into Dance and be amazed!
Fall into Music! Fall into Lyrics! Fall into Sounds of Acoustics!
—But more importantly—
Fall into His Amazing Grace—the loving arms of God!

SALVATION

See, God has come to save me! I will trust and not be afraid,
for the Lord is my strength and song; He is my Salvation.
Isaiah 12:2 (TLB)

I hope this book touched you in some way, shape, or form. No one is perfect but God! The most precious and beautiful thing about God is that His heart is wide open to receive us. He gave His Son as an indescribable gift. We may not always think about the depth of this indescribable gift which is the beauty of a perfect atonement. If you feel led to pray the Salvation prayer—Praise God and welcome to the family. This gift is yours for free, should you open your heart to receive it.

═══ SALVATION PRAYER ═══

If you declare with your mouth, "Jesus is Lord," and believe in your heart that God raised him from the dead, you will be saved. For it is with your heart that you believe and are justified, and it is with your mouth that you profess your faith and are saved—Romans 10:9-10 (NIV).

Give your love to God. Give your heart to God. Give your all to God, after all, He gave His all to you when He gave you His only begotten Son. Please email me at (adamslisamarie@aol.com) if you pray this *Salvation* prayer. It would be a blessing to see if this book has touched anyone's heart.

In closing: *May God, the source of hope, fill you with joy and peace through your faith in Him. Then you will overflow with hope by the power of the Holy Spirit*—Romans 15:13 (NOG)

Blessings
Lisa Adams
God's beloved—Daughter of Christ

EPILOGUE*

Unconstrained Season

*The Epilogue is a performance that my Sistah girlfriend Nina (Linda) Tillery and I had performed together at the Black Box Theater (MD) and at the Kennedy Center (DC). Nina, a poet at heart came from the cancer perspective and I came from the healing perspective. Nina has been a blessing in my life and I thank God for our friendship. We always work together seamlessly. Enjoy our poetic tapestry!

Announcement
Introducing the undisputed Heavyweight Contender of the world. This Contender is known as the original heavy-hitter with more notches on its belt for winning than losing. This Contender is ferocious and determined to devour everything in its path. This Contender frightens everyone with an explosive called the c-bomb. This Contender loathes all its victims. This Contender's name is "C" better known as the "Big C." Steer clear or you may be its next casualty.

******

Greetings
I am "**C**," the invincible me
Nothing can stop me
They call me the "**Big C**"
Better known as **cancer**, yep, that's me
There are over 100 of us, you see
All rolled up to a common word call **cancer** or the "**Big C**"
My family is large, larger than you think
When you're diagnosed with the "**Big C**"
You'll hold your breath and forget to blink
Let me introduce a few relatives of mine
Maybe you've heard of a **cancer** of another kind
Fibrocystic, more common in women and found in the breast
Prostrate can be found in both, but more common to men, no less
Esophageal, Bronchogenic Carcinomas, and Acute Myeloid Leukemia
Are **cancers** from smoking, just to name a few
Even second-hand smoking is just as bad
I would get myself check if I were you
There is no limit to gender or origin to which I will attack
The longer you wait for a diagnosis
The strength of treatment is slack
I am family-oriented and I don't discriminate against others
I will attack your cousins, aunts and uncles,
sisters, fathers, brothers, and mothers
I like them all but the feeling is not mutual
To try and kill me, you need radiation and chemo
You know the usual
Some of you go into remission and some of you won't
Makes no difference to me, I just move on
The pain is crucial, very hard to withstand
I'll treat you unfairly, as no other disease can
Slowly but surely, you'll lose some of all your hair
Spend all day in bed, cause you can't sit in a chair
Lose plenty of weight because your appetite is not there
Yes, I am the least liked of many diseases

I do my job well to keep you ill at ease
I would like to apologize for the horror you go thru
But it's out of my control, it's just what I do

Author Nina Tillery | Poems from the Heart, 2020

******

Memo Response
To: **"Big C"** and its entire family

I will admit that the experience that I encountered with "C"
Had me completely topsy-turvy
My initial response was fear and anger
Alarms went off, yelling danger, danger
Everyone told me to beware
I heeded their advice because I was scared
I was very sad that is true
I was at my lowest feeling blue
The diagnosis had me upset
I was given five years on a bet
> A bet that I would not survive for long
> A bet that death would surely come
> A bet that I would lose the battle
> A bet that the stress—I would not be able to handle
The odds of the bets were against me
I took those odds to my Father in prayer, you see
No weapon formed against me shall prosper
That is what my Dad said and I am His daughter
> The bet was blocked as it tried to attack
> The bet was annihilated in its tracks
> The bet was lost against all odds
> The bet was defeated by Almighty God
I believe every Word from my Father
My Rock, my Refuge, My Provider

I did not have to fear the "Big C"
I only had to trust in the "**Real C**"
The "**Real C**" is **Christ** indeed
The only **One sure bet for me!**

******

The following is short poetic story about cancer. I referred to cancer as "*that thing*." Although the story is about cancer, it can be about any disease such as MS (Multiple Sclerosis), Sarcoidosis, Lou Gehrig, Depression, or whatever. As you read the story, everywhere you see "*that thing*" insert your circumstance. The enemy wants you out for the count, but God wants you to trust and believe. If you are still struggling, ask God to help you with your unbelief (see Mark 9:24). God is the Great I AM, Jehovah Rapha—our healer! He is faithful!

******

That Thing

Petrified! I was shaken and scared! What is "*that thing*?" This cannot be! This haunting image began to take hold of me and was strangling my thoughts. I needed air! I could not breathe. The light of life was waning from me. What do I do? Oh no, the mountain of fear stood over me 100 feet tall and kept growing bigger and bigger and closing over my mind. I was so scared. The fear came rushing towards me with full force. It began to spread like butter across my mind. The butter seeped quickly onto the spongy toast of my emotions. Seeping deeper into the depths of my soul. I was stuck between assumptions and presumptions. I skirted the borders of tremors and collided with the jolts and jerks of an out-of-control roller coaster. No, I thought to myself, this cannot be! My emotions began to grow like a gigantic poisonous weed taking over the beautiful, serene gardens of my once peaceful mind. My emotions became *unstable, unsettled, unpredictable.* My emotions were exploding and crackling like loose dangerous wires. They were shooting off like fireworks . . . blowing up but going nowhere. This gloomy ill-faded shadow quickly hastened me into a state of severe **Panic**.

Panic came over me like the flood of an unexpected heavy downpour of a fierce rainstorm. *"that thing"* had me drenched in terror. It triggered the emotion of anxiety which pounded and crashed against the synapses of my brain. The cells of my brain began to swell at the thought of such unwelcoming facts. Am I awake? Is this a dream? Wait, let me pinch myself. No, this is real! Surreal! It's sooooo real! It felt like I had been sucker-punched and blindsided at the same time. I was drowning in the abyss of what-ifs. The what-ifs began choking me as I read the gagging statistics that stared back at me. I plunged deeper into the murky mires of my thoughts and I felt uneasy and disquieted. I sank deeply into my mind of unhealthy apprehension. My sanity began to slip away as I slid down the wall into a fetal position crying, crying, and crying uncontrollably. *Shaken! Sad! Scared!* My thoughts ping-ponged back and forth, back and forth and forth and back. My heart, mind, body, and soul united on one twisted accord. A twisted accord strumming to the beat of uncertainty and overshadowing my mind with ambiguous thoughts of abandoned hope. This abandoned hope had me **Perplexed**.

Perplexed was the driveway that I parked on, off baffle street. *"That thing"* was destined to annihilate all opponents in its path. It was a hurricane aligned to pull my soul into the whirlwind of anguish. *Bewildered! Bemused! Confused!* I feared that it would drown me like a gigantic tsunami riding upon the Pacific Ocean. But I could not shake it. I tried but it kept haunting me during the sunshine of the day and whispering eerie dreadful thoughts under the moonlit skies of the night. I could not escape the out-of-control train that was speeding along the tracks of my thoughts. This train was destined to wreck. I had to get off before I lose my mind completely. But how? How do I get off of this speeding contraption? I began to rub my aching temple with my index finger in a circular motion around, and around, and around again. I could not think! I needed to! Oh, no! Instinctively a darkened black shadow cast over me and engulfed my entire body with unfathomable **Pain**.

Pain is what I am feeling right now because of *"that thing."* Deep down in the core of my soul is a pain that I cannot shake. A brittle scream of shattering glass broke into a thousand pieces on the floor. Each piece represents some part of my life. My mind is spinning in a ball of confusion. I was thinking to myself, what is happening? I scream out to deafening ears to no one, someone, anyone...yet all I got was the dead silence of no answer. Ironically, I heard a loud ringing sound clanging against every morsel of my body and writhing in a torrential outpour of agony. All I am feeling right now is extreme pain from *hurt, distress, and misery!* The painful hurt of a splinter in your finger that you cannot get to. The painful distress of an unanswered question that keeps you jammed locked in a state of worry. The painful misery that keeps your emotions below sea level where you cannot breathe. You become drowned by the undercurrent of life in and out of the water. All I am feeling right now is pain, hurt, distress, and misery; pain, hurt, distress, and misery; pain, hurt, distress, and misery! I could not stop the echo. I tried to silence them, and I became even more frustrated and that frustration grew into a ferocious fiery fury. The fury in me exploded and set off my already irritated temporal mood to just being downright **Piqued**.

Piqued*! "That thing"* had me piqued to point of **piquedtivity**! I hurled an object across the room as if to relieve some stress and I accidentally cracked a vase. Well, maybe it wasn't accidentally—someone, something needs to feel my emotions of being piqued. The vase ideally represented the state of my mind. *Cracked! Broken! Shattered!* Cracked from the shock of the untimely report. Broken from the horrid statistical news that the report rendered. Shattered from the uncontrollable thoughts that I cannot put in check nor grasp hold onto. I just could not wrap my mind around all that was happening to me. I was balled up in a twisted knot with nowhere to turn. There was no escape! I had to flee! Where can I go? Where can I run? I cannot move. I felt closed in. I felt stuck!

I was frozen in time and space. Needing to move but I couldn't. My emotions were steaming hot like a boiling tea kettle on a stove. I needed to cool down. I stopped for a moment and pondered about the state of my mind. That ponder turned to irritation and that irritation infuriated me. The more I thought about it, the more infuriated I became. I stopped my run-away thoughts and looked directly at the monstrosity that was before me. In an authoritative voice, I demanded an answer to the question, who even gave you **Permission**?

Permission? Who gave *"that thing"* permission? Who authorized this fear in my life? I do not have to answer your call! Something, rose inside of me to become bold and indignant as I spoke to this *despicable, disgusting, and deadly* fear that was hovering over me like a helicopter. Who gave you the license to notarize illegal documents and seal them with trepidation and fear? Who gave you the consent to impose apprehensive signals of distress? Who gave you the position to deposit and plant seeds of *dread, despair, and terror*? I never called on you! I never desired you! I loathe you with the deepest despise. You are detestable and I abhor you. And the worst part is I never saw you coming. You crept up on me like the poisonous venomous snake that you are. I want to know why you are here invading my space without my permission. How did you get through the door of my heart? I did not hear you knock. I would have never answered because you are not welcome here. You are never, ever, ever welcome here! Do you hear that echo reverberating across the mountains of my heart? Skipping to the rhythmic sounds of never, ever, never, ever. I did not give you permission to tread on my territory. This is my space, not yours. I demand to know why are you here without my permission? Hello? All I heard was silence! Ummmm, this is a **Problem**.

Problem? *"That thing"* had become an intrusive problem. I began to pick the problem apart like a seventh-grader working diligently dissecting a frog in a school lab. I needed this problem to be solved. The problem with the problem that gave me problems was that the problem needed to be solved and that was the problem. The problem had too many faces, yet no mouth to speak or tongue to answer. This problem was disguised as massively complicated, stressfully debilitating, and mind-boggling devastating. It masterminded terror around every probable solution that I uttered. I loathed its despicable attacks. I detested its sneaky no less deadly ways. I abhorred that it lurked in the deepest crevices of my soul and I wanted it to be evicted from mine. I needed to erase *"that thing"* from the blackboard of my mind. I declared, "that's it!" No more chalk for you to write those *detrimental, degrading, disavowing* words again. Uuuuurgh, I got to solve this, but nothing was adding up. I became so infuriated because it showed right back up again. The infuriation had me spiraling downward rapidly into the quicksand of no return. I began gasping for breath as I was looking for something to hold onto. I grabbed hold of myself and the reflection I saw was my debilitating self-made **Prison.**

Prison? *"That thing"* had me in prison! Not the local penitentiary but the prison of *doubt, fear, and trepidation.* Did I do this to myself? How did I even get here? My mind was whirling around like batter being mixed in a bowl swirling in the combinations of dark and light at the makings of a marble cake. I felt the battle between dark and light and it was a personal struggle of tug-of-war. I needed to escape. I realized that the self-made prison had been my selective choice of food. I feared everything about this imposter. And that fear left me *weak, frail, and helpless.* This ferocious monstrosity came unannounced and imbedded itself on me like a blood-sucking leech that it was. It was the abomination lurking to destroy every fiber of my being. I did not like this self-made prison. The prison walls were closing in on me and I felt claustrophobic. I stretched out my arms and ended up grabbing onto the bars of distress and hopelessness and began sinking to the prison cell floor of my life. I tried to shake myself loose. I began frantically shaking the iron-clad bars of my heart, my mind, my body, and my soul. I thought about this intruder morning, noon, and night. I could not break free of the chains that kept me drowning in the sea of fear and the depths of despair. The tentacles of poison were strapped onto me tightly and the more I tried to fight the tighter the grip became. I tried over and over to break free. I was so distraught that I did not realize that I had boxed myself into becoming a self-made prisoner inside of my thoughts. Its venom seeped its way into the depths of my soul. I was determined to break free. I reached out to grab a hold of something *empowering, encouraging, or uplifting* but I could not hold onto them. They slipped through my fingers like a scoop of sand along the Chesapeake Bay Shores. I was courted again by the trifles of my anxiety. It held me close and we danced the tango . . . da, da, da, da, da. We walked together and I allowed it to snuggle up to my bosom, da, da, da, da, da. I felt the stronghold pulling me in tighter and tighter. Wait! No! Not this time. I stopped and refused to finish the dance. I decided the tango needed a change-o. Instinctively, a sweet melodic essence came over me to **Pray.**

Pray, yes, that's it! *"That thing"* had me topsy-turvy and I was doing everything but praying. I had realized that prayer had been the one truth that had alluded me. I was entangled at the ballpark of self-defeat. I was entwined with *fear, doubts, and struggles.* I was sullenly engrossed in the dugout of my pity party. As I humbly began to pray, God opened my eyes to see heavens army of angels on the outfield. *Purity* brought the team together to huddle on how to best position ourselves. *Purity* provided a strategy and declared to only believe that everything was as it should be and to trust His direction. *My Shield* was my left fielder, *My Sword* was my right fielder, and *My Armor* was cloaked centerfield. *Purity* explained that it may appear that the opposition is winning, but for me to turn my focus upon Him only. *Watch, learn, and believe* that I AM. I AM all that is possible. The crowd grew loud with jeering from the opponents and cheering from the allies. The bases were loaded. Pity was up to bat. Poison was on first; Pretense was on second, and Parasite was on third. *Purity,* which was poised with grace, mercy, and love stepped onto the pitcher's mound. Purity got into his pitcher stance, hiked up His leg, and windup His arm to spin a mean curveball. The powerhouse CURVEBALL thrown was a—strike one. Pity had swung and missed. Pity decided to try again. *Purity* turned the baseball cap and—swoosh. The angelic referee announced—strike two. Pity was mad and getting angrier by the second. Pity tightened his grip on the bat, hit the ground a couple of times determined not to let me forget that poison that he intentionally planted in the recesses of my mind. This was his final attempt to annihilate me, his opponent. The enemies camp motioned to each other a strategy to take out the opposition for good. *Purity* pulled the cap forward, signaled to the umpire, hiked up that leg, windup His arm; and this time he threw a DROP PITCH and that completely confused Pity as he swung his bat in sheer defeat. The referee bellowed out—strike three, game over! The conquest has been defeated. I repeat the conquest has been defeated. NaNaNaNa, NaNaNaNa—hey-hey-hey, good-bye. NaNaNaNa, NaNaNaNa—hey-hey-hey, I won!

****

We are all on this field called life where we will encounter various attacks from the adversary. God is our battle fighter. Our **most powerful weapon** against our adversary is **PRAYER! Prayers give us the Victor's Crown**. Keep in step with prayer which will align and connect you directly to the Heavenly Father. It is vital to develop a lifestyle *Attitude of Prayer* or as one lady coined it:

"Prayeritude."

Always remember that PRAYER is a privilege opportunity to have a divine connection with God—don't miss it!

P–Petitioning
R–Requests
A–Activates
Y–Yahweh's hand

The End!

First time Author
Seeking to share His glory!

Printed in the United States
by Baker & Taylor Publisher Services